BEAST

OF NEW CASTLE

THE HEART-POUNDING BATTLE TO STOP A SAVAGE KILLER

LARRY SELLS
MARGIE PORTER

WILDBLUE
PRESS

WildBluePress.com

BEAST OF NEW CASTLE published by:
WILDBLUE PRESS
P.O. Box 102440
Denver, Colorado 80250

WILDBLUE PRESS is registered at the U.S. Patent and Trademark Offices.

ISBN 978-1-948239-66-0 Trade Paperback
ISBN 978-1-948239-65-3 eBook

Cover design © 2019 WildBlue Press. All rights reserved.

Interior Formatting/Book Cover Design by Elijah Toten
www.totencreative.com

BEAST

OF NEW CASTLE

TABLE OF CONTENTS

CHAPTER 1—A MURDER IN NEW CASTLE

The murder weapon was a sawed-off shotgun, seven pounds of thunder that could churn a man's skull into applesauce. On February 12, 1991, Shawn McCormick, a hard-looking woman with no criminal record, purchased the 12 gauge shotgun at a Kmart in New Castle, Indiana. Tall and a bit heavy, Shawn's average appearance was easily forgotten by store personnel.

The shotgun would be etched into the town's history.

Shawn told Kmart clerk LaWanna DuVall that she was going rabbit hunting; but it turned out that the cottontails of the wild were safe. Instead of prowling the woods for game, Shawn placed the shotgun in the hands of her big, bad boyfriend, Jerry K. Thompson.

Thompson had served time for two counts of auto theft. Now a free man, he was determined to do as he pleased and McCormick was a woman who would do anything he asked.

That February, five months after he walked out of prison, Thompson was on probation, and guidelines stated that Thompson could neither carry nor purchase a firearm. But that was just somebody else's lame rule—it didn't mean he couldn't have a gun. He told Shawn exactly what type of gun and which ammunition to buy. Jerry Thompson was in a mood to do some shooting.

With its three-inch shells, the gun was an impressive weapon. Thompson could shoot a gun this powerful and not blink twice. Yes, the murder weapon was perfect for a man like Jerry Thompson.

The thirty-one-year-old didn't look like he needed a gun to protect himself. Towering six feet five and topping 300 pounds, Thompson was a beast of a man. When angered his face bore a countenance of cruelty. His blue eyes appeared black and soulless when he was enraged.

His skin, neck to toes, was a tattooed declaration of his belief in white supremacy and his hatred for all men of color. A large Aryan cross tattoo plastered his neck. In prison, it was a dare. Although the Aryan Brotherhood accounts for less than 1 percent of the American prison population, they stand accused of up to 20 percent of prison murders.

Thompson did not wear his ink lightly. It was reported that, while in prison, Thompson had an encounter with his dark-skinned cellmates. He wanted to watch the Country Music Awards. They wanted to watch MTV. Thompson came out swinging at the twelve convicts who refused to see things his way. He put four of them in the hospital. The rest he clobbered hard enough to ensure that he got to watch his program.

An enraged lion, the Beast was prepared to pounce on anyone who crossed him. Another prisoner had the job of "enforcer." Prison is a locked down community and like any group of people, convicts have their pecking order. The enforcer beat down anyone who refused tribute to the prison boss. His ego was displayed across his back, a dinner-plate-sized gang tattoo. Thompson demanded the enforcer's job and was refused. So, Thompson threw the man down and scalped the tattoo from his flesh. He became the new enforcer, exacting tribute from others and claiming his share of the take. Later he sewed the man's tattooed skin onto the back of his motorcycle jacket.

Thompson began mud wrestling with the law at age twelve. He made friends with marijuana at age thirteen. He was also fond of beer, Dark Eyes vodka, cocaine, heroin,

PCP, acid, and crack. It was rumored that in his youth he killed an elderly woman.

Since the day he was paroled from prison, September 9, 1990, Thompson had failed to find work. His girlfriend, Shawn, worked third shift at a Shell station and he supplemented their income with the proceeds of stolen cars and drug deals.

He would be discharged from parole on July 24, 1991, five months after the Crandall murder. The state parole agent who autographed the papers could never have guessed that he was signing permission for a bloodthirsty killer to prowl the streets. Thompson's seven prior felonies should have given him a clue. The man had served time for two thefts, burglary, battery, rape, child molestation, and escape.

Thompson would later claim that he didn't know Shawn had bought him a gun. He said he refused it because it was a violation of his probation to have the weapon, and that he gave it to his friend and partner in crime, Douglas Percy.

Percy's garage was a carnival of tools that included acetylene torches and grinders. He purchased the dye Thompson would use for camouflage when he sawed off the barrel and stock of the shotgun. The pair designed a sling for the weapon so they could more easily conceal it beneath their coats.

Two days after Shawn made her Kmart purchase, her main man had the perfect, easily concealed weapon. Happy Valentine's Day.

A few hours before the murder Thompson and Percy drove to an area called Spiceland Pike near New Castle. They pulled off the highway, parked Thompson's orange-yellow pickup truck and hiked up a hill into a wooded area where they test-fired the gun.

After shooting the weapon several times and finding it satisfactory, Thompson drove through a park where he slid off the road and got stuck. Once they freed the wheels the two drove on and stopped at a liquor store for beer and cigarettes.

Just a couple of guys hanging out.

The liquor store was on a main road and had a canopy over it like a drive-through diner. Thompson stayed in the truck, handing Percy twenty dollars for their purchases. When Percy returned Thompson let him keep the change and gave him an additional twenty, telling him that it was his part of the take.

"For what?" Percy wondered.

"For what we're gonna do."

Wesley W. Crandall Jr., age forty, was a small-time drug dealer and self-employed apartment manager. His apartment house at 1218 South 18th Street in New Castle, Indiana, was definitely a fixer-upper, but he called it home. His friends dubbed him "Junior" and they knew where to find him.

The front door to Crandall's home led into a hallway with apartments on the left and right. Crandall slept in the apartment on the right. The one across the hall, on the north side, stood unoccupied. Crandall stored marijuana in the refrigerator of the empty apartment. The stairs led up to another apartment, also empty.

Crandall's friends stated that recently he had become a cautious man. His home had been broken into and money stolen a couple of weeks prior. Crandall suspected one of his friends, a man named Charlie Alcorn, of the theft. Crandall was known to keep vast amounts of marijuana in his home. He also kept guns and pit bulls; he had a reputation for being "schizoid."

In early January 1991, a mutual friend, Davey Loveless, introduced Thompson's brother David to Crandall. Both Jerry and David Thompson soon began buying marijuana from Crandall. To Wesley Crandall, Jerry Thompson was just another welcome customer, a man he would readily invite into his home.

Early evening on Valentine's Day brought fog. The temperature hovered in the mid-twenties but felt five degrees colder, the chill accentuated with rain and light blowing snow. Thompson and Percy made a trip to Crandall's house to get some marijuana.

They parked Thompson's truck at a nearby intersection by a church and approached Crandall's house, a weary two-story structure, staggering off its foundation and wearing a patchwork of wood and ancient sidings.

Another customer, Mark Winchester, was at Crandall's home between 5:30 and 6:00 p.m. that day. When Thompson knocked at the entry door, Crandall told Winchester it was strange. Most of Crandall's friends simply walked into the house and knocked on his apartment door. He went to answer the front door.

Alarmed at being seen buying marijuana, Winchester ducked his head and backed into Crandall's apartment as the two men entered. Then he left hurriedly, squeezing past Thompson and Percy in the narrow hallway. Winchester said he got "the merest glance" at the visitors, "just a fraction of a second."

Crandall's meagerly furnished apartment was an oversized junk drawer. His personal belongings were layered hodgepodge on every flat surface, as if he had no storage cabinets and had simply dumped his life out of some grocery bags. A blue can of refrigerant guarded an ashtray littered with several brands of cigarette butts. The man's entire life: baseball cards, pornography, hats, books…were easily accessible to any casual visitor. A volume of *Pocket Knives & Razors* lay at an angle as if Crandall had stopped reading midsentence. He would never finish the book.

Percy smuggled the shotgun into Crandall's apartment but passed it over to Thompson. His explanation for handing over his only weapon in a drug dealer's house was that he never thought about having to protect himself when he was with the giant. Thompson assured him that, "nothing's going to happen."

Junior Crandall certainly expected that nothing would happen to him. He prescreened the people he allowed in his home and kept his dogs nearby. He was prepared for war. His personal armory, scattered through his home, included a 9mm fully automatic machine pistol, a Smith & Wesson .32, a Colt .32, and a Smith & Wesson .38. He also owned a Taurus 357, two more 9mm pistols, and four .22s. Crandall had a business and he intended to protect it.

It was all business—until Thompson decided to rob and kill Crandall.

Percy lingered in the living room while Thompson stepped into the kitchen to speak with Crandall. The attack came without warning. None of Crandall's weapons could save him from Thompson's fully loaded fist. Standing five feet, eleven inches tall, and weighing 178 pounds, Crandall had no chance in a fight against Thompson.

Percy heard a pumpkin smash thud when Thompson knocked the victim out with a single punch. Then he saw Thompson leap up and come down, stomping on Crandall's head.

Thompson ordered Percy to come into the kitchen and take the bags of marijuana from Crandall's refrigerator. The smaller man entered to find Thompson leaning over Crandall's prone body. "I think I broke his neck," Thompson said.

Crandall's kitchen appliances were diminutive even for an apartment, but they were decades old, heavy, and well-made. Percy tugged the handle on the left side of the refrigerator door and discovered it was broken. He kept yanking, struggling to open the sealed door. Then Thompson left the kitchen and returned with a handgun.

Percy froze when he heard the distinctive click of the gun. But the weapon misfired. Later he would say, "I thought he was shooting at me; he's already knocked this guy out."

Thompson left the kitchen again to fetch a second handgun from another room. Percy was a trapped animal, his racing heart the only proof that he had not died from fright.

The second gun also misfired.

Percy pried the edge of the refrigerator with his fingertips, jerking the handle up, down, left, right, fighting to jimmy the refrigerator door open. The big man yelled at Percy, angry that he had not managed to open the refrigerator and take the marijuana.

Thompson left the kitchen for the third time. Percy battled the obstinate handle as if he smelled his own death coming.

Crandall was still prone on the floor and Percy tried to avert his eyes when Thompson again returned to the kitchen, this time carrying the shotgun and a pillow. Worried that Thompson would shoot him for not opening the refrigerator, Percy kept his eyes hyper focused on the door handle. Then he heard the murderous blast.

Whiffs of gunpowder and the odor of butchery snaked terror through Percy's guts. Blood and brain matter erupted across the bare linoleum floor.

Percy's eyes could not blink away the reality. The gory pillow swathed Crandall's head. It could have been Percy's own skull bursting from beneath blood-soaked cotton and polyester. Keenly aware that Thompson still held the murderous gun, Percy was careful to not react. He realized that in Thompson's mind, he needed to remain as loyal as a lapdog.

The pair forced the refrigerator open and took the stash of marijuana. The refrigerator, now bare except for some butter and a couple of condiments on one shelf stood open and stark, like a victim. They robbed Crandall's apartment, stuffing a white trash bag with the marijuana. They also swiped a few of the guns stowed throughout the apartment, along with some ammunition.

When they left Crandall's home, wintry dusk was fading into a moonless night. They hopped off the porch steps and cut across the grass. Thompson believed they had left no witnesses. His mantra was, "no witnesses, no problems." They carried their loot to Thompson's pickup truck. On the drive home to Percy's house in Indianapolis they discussed their alibis.

CHAPTER 2—DETECTIVE STEPHENS SEEKS A KILLER

Anna Mae Stewart was at home with her son on the evening of the murder. She was watching the clock, timing the child's allotted minutes to play Nintendo. At 6:45 p.m. she heard a knock at the door. A friend, Jeffrey Howe, asked her to go for a ride with him "because something is wrong."

Both Jeff Howe and Anna Stewart rented apartments at 1419 South 17th Street in New Castle; he lived upstairs, she lived downstairs. Junior Crandall was their friend and their landlord.

Howe had gone to Crandall's house to borrow a ladder and some walk boards because "he was gonna do some painting in the apartment we lived in," Stewart said. Howe found both the front screen door and the wooden door into the hall shut but the hallway was dark and both downstairs apartment doors stood wide open. Junior Crandall was nowhere to be seen.

Finding the situation odd, Howe decided to fetch Stewart because she had been friends with Crandall for many years while he had only known his landlord a short while. Howe did not want Crandall to come home and find him in his apartment, especially since the recent break-in.

Stewart had known Crandall for about fifteen years, since she was seventeen years old. At one time she lived with him for a few months in his upstairs apartment. Crandall would not be leery if he saw Stewart in his home. She agreed to go with Howe in his truck. Together they rode the few short blocks to Junior's house.

The icy weather with snow on the ground gave their landlord's house a stark, forlorn look. Entering, Stewart found things just as Howe had described, the hallway dark and lifeless, both apartment doors gaped open. Crandall's apartment was also dark. Stewart saw nothing unusual at first. Her friend's living quarters were always filthy, smelling of old urine and dog feces.

The single light that had been left on, a kitchen bulb, illuminated the crime scene. Anna Stewart did not enter the kitchen. She crept just close enough to glimpse Junior's arm and some blood on the floor. Alarmed, she began pushing Howe out. "Whoever's done this could still be in here," she explained later. "I don't know why; I just had that feeling."

Fearing the worst, the two made their way to the front door. "And he went down the hallway and I kind of bounced around the hallway because I was bumping into the sides of the wall because it was so dark, I couldn't see where I was going. And then we went out and jumped in the truck," Stewart said.

Stewart's first thought was that they needed to call an ambulance. She and Howe drove a few blocks to the nearest phone at Jerry's Super Val. On the drive they must have realized the truth. When they reached the store, they had the clerk in the office call for police instead of an ambulance. They wanted to report that their friend Junior Crandall had been murdered.

Returning to the house, Stewart and Howe parked across the street and waited for the police to arrive.

***

At 6:45 p.m., New Castle police received a call from Anna Stewart, a friend of Crandall's. She and another friend had discovered his body, lying prone on the kitchen floor.

The two officers who responded to the call, Ross Frame and Allen Criswell, found the body clad in faded denim jeans and a black leather jacket. A blood-drenched pillow shrouded what had once been his face and covered a mass of dark, shoulder length, wavy locks. Crandall's pit bulls were shut into the bedroom.

Officer Frame lifted the pillow with its Garfield cartoon pillowcase off of Crandall's head and checked for vital signs. Finding no signs of life and no weapon, Frame and Criswell called for the homicide investigation team.

Detective Captain James R. "Jim" Stephens arrived on the scene at 7:15 p.m. and spoke with Investigator Ernie Crabtree of the New Castle Police Department. Stephens reported, "I stepped to the kitchen door and looked in and observed a white male lying on his stomach with his face pointing towards the front of the kitchen stove. I noticed what appeared to be brain matter on the bottom of the stove, on the left arm of the deceased on the floor. I also noticed a large blood loss."

The blood-engorged pillow lay on newspapers stacked on top of a cardboard barrel. Stephens called Officer Frame to confirm that he had moved it.

The shell had exploded through the pillow and into Crandall's left temple. The exit wound was a three-inch starburst through the victim's forehead from the bridge of his nose upward. His eyes, still attached to the base of his skull by connective tissue, had erupted through the wound.

Crandall's wallet, which contained no money, lay on the floor to his right along with a plastic photo insert. His license had been removed to help with identification. Stephens also noted a spent 9mm casing just inside the kitchen door.

Stewart was familiar with Crandall's guns. She told investigators that "there was always weapons laying around because it made me nervous, I mean piled up guns on the table, at the end of his bed there in the living room…all I know is he had a 9mm. It looked something like a machine gun."

Stewart confessed to knowing little about guns but said, "He had a black handgun I think for a while that he laid on the coffee table but I don't remember seeing it lately and then he had a handgun that he carried on him in a shoulder holster. All I know is a handgun and it was black and brown. It looked kind of big to me to be carrying on a person."

Besides having pit bulls, Crandall truly was well-armed against intruders. While investigating his murder, Detective Ed Davis listed a Taurus stainless steel revolver and a .357 with a ribbed barrel and wood grips on top of the dresser in the west room of the apartment along the north wall. The revolver was empty.

A blue gun box on the coffee table in the living room contained a Jennings .22 caliber semi-automatic pistol and magazine. This pistol was also empty. The coffee table also held a folding knife with gold lettering spelling out "Cougar" along the wooden handle. A switchblade with a blue handle laid on the coffee table near it.

On the bed in the living room was a gray plastic pistol box.

Leaning against the living room wall on the south side of the door leading into the kitchen was a Ruger .22 caliber semi-automatic rifle with a telescopic sight. There was no magazine and the chamber was empty.

Braced against the same wall was a Stevens single shot, drop action shotgun, loaded with a Winchester 12 gauge shell from which the lead shot had been removed and replaced, apparently, with salt.

Anna Stewart did not seem to think that the home had been vandalized. Crandall's apartment, she said, was typically dirty and chaotic. "I mean you was lucky to find a place to sit down. Most of the time when I went over there, I didn't sit down."

Stewart knew that Crandall kept marijuana in the apartment. She said it was in his kitchen in the top drawer by the stove, and also in the unoccupied apartment on the left inside a green refrigerator. Also, "He always carried a lot of money on him."

The Henry County Homicide Investigation Team's initial report said that, pending autopsy, the cause of Crandall's death was a head wound caused by single shotgun blast. Detective Stephens told reporters that police would be interviewing friends or neighbors in hopes of finding someone who heard or saw something.

Officer Ross Frame left the investigation in the hands of the homicide team and departed from Crandall's home to survey the neighborhood. He knocked on neighbors' doors to learn what, if anything, they had seen.

Crandall's twenty-one-year-old neighbor, Mrs. Gladys Catherine Case, gave her statement to Frame. She lived diagonally across the street from Crandall. She said she saw a person she referred to as "Wolfman," leave Crandall's house carrying what looked like a white trash bag. She said another man carried something long, that looked like a gun, in a concealed manner. After speaking with Frame, she was taken to the New Castle Police Station to repeat her statement to Detective Sergeant Kim Cronk and Sergeant Harold Griffin.

It appeared that the two killers had walked away clean, but they had been seen. Mark Winchester had seen them arrive and Mrs. Case had seen them leave. Mrs. Case never heard the blast that ended Crandall's life but she seemed eager to tell law enforcement exactly what she saw. She offered investigators several volunteer statements. Winchester would take a few days to think about it.

When Gladys Case heard of the death, her first thought was that Crandall had been attacked by his dogs. She had seen the pit bulls, of course; she was in the habit of watching Crandall's apartment house. Married and the mother of two young children, she was concerned about the number of people who carried guns into and out of the residence.

On the evening of February 14, Mrs. Case said she was getting into her car to drive to the Val Department Store to buy Valentine candy for the children. Between 5:30 and 6:00 p.m. she saw two men leave Crandall's house and walk away across the grass. One of them, she said, carried a white trash bag cradled in his arms like a baby. The bag appeared to be filled with "red and green stuff," she said.

Mrs. Case told Sergeant Cronk that she recognized the smaller man. He was a local known as "Wolfman," Ralph Jacobs Jr., age thirty. Mrs. Case said that she saw the Wolfman in the area "about every other day," and knew him well on sight. He was easily identified, she said, because he had a dark mane of hair and a humped back.

Wolfman, she said, was wearing a light brown coat, one he frequently wore. She did not claim to know the other man who left with Wolfman but described him as having black hair, a black mustache, and possibly a beard.

Mrs. Case identified Ralph Jacobs's picture in a photo array. Police immediately began trawling local bars in search of the Wolfman.

Stephens's report, dated February 14, 1991, at 7:15 p.m. described the search.

He wrote that, after receiving information about what Gladys Case had seen, "myself and Deputy Chief Pinkerton decided to check some of the bars for a man I knew as Ralph Jacobs AKA [sic] 'Wolfman.' We left the crime scene and drove first to 647 North Main Street to the Jacobs home. The lights were on but we elected not to stop until we checked to see if he was out running around.

"We left there and drove out to Whiskey River, a bar located in the 1400 block of Broad Street and another bar called Chuck's Place also in the 1400 block of Broad Street.

The suspect was not at either place. We left there and started to the Bamboo and as we got back to the homicide scene, we observed State Police Investigator Ed Davis, a homicide team member, standing outside so we stopped and picked him up.

"The three of us continued checking the bars. We stopped first at the Bamboo and then a place called the Twilight Club; neither turned up anything of significance at this time. After checking all these places, we decided to go back to the home of Ralph "Wolfman" Jacobs and see if he was home so as to bring him in for questioning.

"We knocked at the door which was answered by Ralph Jacobs. I identified myself and the officers with me as Police Officers and asked Mr. Jacobs if he would mind coming to the Police Station to talk to us. Ralph replied yes, but I've been home all evening, in fact I've been here all day.

"Mr. Ralph Jacobs Sr., who by now had come to the door said, 'That's right, he's been here all day, he hasn't been off the place.' I explained to them that we were making an investigation into a death and still needed to talk to him to which he, Ralph Jr., said, 'Let me get my coat.'

"Ralph got his coat on and we left and were just getting into the car and Ralph said again, 'I've been home all day except for going to the North End Market, you can check with the owner and he will tell you I was there.'"

At 9:30 p.m. they arrived at the police station. Questioned for several hours, Ralph Jacobs remained cooperative but insisted he did not know Crandall and had no information about his murder.

When he signed an Interrogation-Advice of Rights form he was incapable of understanding the full meaning of the rights he was signing away and what it meant to relinquish those rights. He didn't think it would matter. He told the investigators plainly that he knew nothing about the crime. No formal statement was taken and no tapes were made.

After about thirty minutes officers returned Jacobs to his home.

The next day, on February 15, 1991, officers returned to the Jacobs home. They had more questions. Would Ralph accompany them to police headquarters? Ralph agreed to go. Again, he was presented with an Advice of Rights forms. Stephens said later that he read the forms to Ralph and that Ralph also read them before he signed.

Stephens interviewed Ralph for about ten minutes. Then he made a seven-minute tape on which Jacobs made a statement denying any knowledge of the crime. He also stated that he had read and understood his Miranda rights and had willingly signed a waiver of those rights.

CHAPTER 3—DEAD MEN TELL

The earthly remains of Junior Crandall were zippered into a body bag and turned over to Henry County Deputy Coroner Bill Palmer. K&W Ambulance Service took the body to the Henry County Hospital morgue for keeping until an autopsy could be scheduled. It would be Palmer's task to deliver the body for that autopsy.

Palmer escorted Crandall's body to the Indiana University School of Medicine Department of Pathology. Initial x-rays of Crandall's head, chest, and abdomen were taken while the body was still in the bag. The autopsy was then delayed because these x-rays suggested possible explosives, so no one was allowed to touch the body until it was declared safe. The questionable objects turned out to be coins and gun shells in Crandall's pockets.

Asked to identify the deceased, Stephens said that he had talked to Crandall on occasion but, "looking at him it was impossible to do this as the blast from the shotgun had removed a large portion of his face." Crandall was identified by comparing his postmortem fingerprints to those on his application for a handgun permit.

Dean A. Hawley, MD, performed the autopsy in the presence of six witnesses including Bill Palmer and Jim Stephens. He received the body still face down and fully clothed. The victim was wearing a black jacket, a sweatshirt, jeans, undershorts, shoes, and socks. Dr. Hawley found $519.53 in cash in Crandall's outside left jacket pocket. He reported that, "The outside jacket pocket also contains a plastic bag full of bullets and coins, a plastic bag of brown leafy material, and a blue condom that contains a scant residue of white powder."

An inside pocket on the left side of Crandall's jacket contained an additional $860 in cash, a checkbook, a lottery ticket apparently worth one dollar, cigarettes, a cigarette lighter, two sets of keys, and "other items not inventoried in this report." Coroner Palmer was given custody of Crandall's property. The money was turned over to Jim Stephens.

Thompson and Percy had walked away with some weed and some weapons but they left behind over $1,379 in Crandall's pockets.

Dr. Hawley described Crandall as a well-developed and well-nourished white male aged forty-one. In fact, Crandall was forty, having died two months before his April 27th birthday.

Except for the barbaric shattering of his skull, Crandall appeared to be in prime health. He was almost six feet tall and weighed nearly 200 pounds. The medical examination netted no traces of alcohol or drugs in the victim's body. No scars, tattoos, or deforming injuries were found. His skin was not jaundiced. His ears were not pierced. Crandall's hair was long and dark brown with some balding on his forehead. He had a beard and mustache.

Crandall had the heart of an athlete. His lungs, kidneys, liver, and digestive system could have been used as illustrations in a health book. He had aspirated no blood. The sole physical problem noted by Dr. Hawley was, "Oral hygiene is poor."

A gaping five-inch split from the front of Crandall's ear to the top of his head marked the entry wound. The plastic shot cup and constellations of pellets were retained inside Crandall's skull, enmeshed in his remaining brain tissue. His teeth were attached to loose fragments of his upper and lower jaws. Dr. Hawley said that his dangling eyes appeared to be hazel.

With Dr. Hawley's signature, gunshot wound to the head became the official cause of death.

OBITUARY

Wesley Wayne Crandall Jr., 40, of 1218 S. 18th Street., New Castle, died of a gunshot wound Thursday, Feb. 14 in his home. An inquiry into his death is being conducted by members of the Henry County Homicide Investigation Team.

He was a native of Henry County, born April 27, 1950, a son of Wesley Wayne Crandall Sr. and Lucy Crandall. He was a self-employed apartment manager.

Survivors include two sisters, Veneda Bush of New Castle and Judith (Mrs. James) Steinbacher of Fort Wayne: and several nieces and nephews.

He was preceded in death by his parents and one brother, Charles Everett Crandall.

Services will be 2 p.m. Wednesday at the Main and Frame Funeral Home with the Rev. Daniel Clemens officiating. Burial will follow in the Mount Summit Cemetery. Friends may call from 3 to 5 and 7 to 9 p.m. Tuesday at the funeral home.

After Crandall's autopsy, Stephens returned to the police station at about 5:10 p.m. on February 15. There was a message for Stephens and Ed Davis from another witness, a friend of Crandall's named Frank Barber. "Mr. Barber said that he knew the deceased very well," Stephens reported, "as he had been to his home on several occasions and he to Junior's home.

"Additionally, Junior had been to his home just before his murder and told him that he suspected Charlie Alcorn as being the one who had broken into his home two weeks prior. He also said that Harold Anderson had taken Junior for $5,000 on a dope buy he was making for Junior. He said Charlie Alcorn had taken ten pounds of pot.

"After hearing the above, I asked Mr. Barber if he had ever been to Junior Crandall's whenever other people were present. Mr. Barber said that he had seen several people there. I showed Mr. Barber a photo array of several people including the picture of Ralph Jacobs. Mr. Barber picked out the picture of Ralph 'Wolfman' Jacobs without any trouble. When asked if he had seen him more than once, Mr. Barber said he had seen him there many times because he used to pick up a boy who lived there in one of the apartments that worked for him and he would see Ralph there when he would drop this boy off. This boy he believed was David Fitzpatrick."

One of the last people to speak with Crandall before his murder was his friend, Mike Dishman. The two had talked on the phone about 3:00 p.m. that day. Dishman said that Crandall seemed normal and not particularly worried. He also told Stephens that he frequently saw people going in and out of Junior's home.

Stephens asked him to look at photographs to see if he recognized anyone. Stephens reported, "Mr. Dishman looked and pointed right away to Ralph Jacobs. I asked him if Ralph went by any other name. Mr. Dishman said everyone knows him as Wolfman. Additionally, Mr. Dishman said that he had seen Ralph 'Wolfman' Jacobs at Junior's house two weeks earlier."

Armed with this information, Stephens and a fellow officer again went to the Jacobs home the evening of February 15, 1991. They asked Ralph Jacobs to come to the station with them and bring both of his coats.

At the station, Mrs. Case identified Ralph's light brown coat as the one she'd seen him wear the evening of the murder. Ralph again denied knowing the murder victim. Stephens confronted the suspect, saying he had witnesses who had seen him at Crandall's home, and that one had seen him leaving the house that evening. Jacobs demanded to know who said that and when Stephens gave him Mrs. Case's name he said, "I don't know her."

Stephens countered that Frank Barber and Mike Dishman had also seen Jacobs at Crandall's home on numerous occasions.

Learning that Ralph's father was in the hallway, Stephens left Ralph with Investigator Davis and went out to speak with the elder Jacobs. His report read, "I explained to Mr. Jacobs Sr. that I had an eyewitness that could place Ralph at Junior's house and further that Ralph had lied to us about ever being at Junior Crandall's home and I knew that he must be mistaken about when Ralph was home.

"Mr. Jacobs Sr. said he just thought Ralph was home upstairs but that he actually didn't see Ralph all afternoon between the hours of 4:00 p.m. and 7:30 or 8:00 p.m. just before supper."

Stephens returned to inform Ralph that he had no alibi. Ralph said, "Okay, I was there."

About three hours after he was taken to the police station, Ralph Jacobs gave the officers a statement.

CHAPTER 4—WOLFMAN IN CUSTODY

The day Junior Crandall died, Ralph "Wolfman" Jacobs Jr. spent the day playing with his new VCR, watching and recording cartoons on the downstairs television. His mother, Janet Jacobs, joked that he was lying around the living room like a kid with no shirt or shoes on. The day was cold, the cartoons mesmerizing, and Ralph was content to stay in the house with his mother.

His father, Ralph Jacobs Sr. and his uncle, Levi Jacobs, were, as usual, out in the garage tinkering with vehicles. Periodically one of Ralph's brothers-in-law would drop in just to chat, drink beer, or work on their cars. Ralph lived with his parents at 647 N. Main Street in New Castle, occupying two upstairs rooms in their home.

At age two, Ralph suffered from spinal meningitis. His mother blamed the infection for his struggles in the classroom. The disease also left him with a humped back and a limited ability to lift heavy items. Ralph had attended four schools and obtained a seventh-grade education. He was expelled from school because he took a swing at a teacher.

Ralph's mother said, "Now all the kids that were there told me, it was the teacher's swing on Ralph first." It didn't matter. The boy's public-school education was ended.

Janet Jacobs claimed that her son could read but it took him awhile to figure things out. Ralph also insisted that he could read and write. Later testing would demonstrate that he could do neither.

Locals nicknamed Ralph "Wolfman" for his long thick mane of hair. He was frequently seen walking all over town. Ralph did not drive. He had one good friend named Wayne Daniels, a cornstalk of a man who occasionally drove a pickup truck. Most of the time, the two walked around town or caught a ride out to the truck stop on the highway. Here they would enjoy coffee or possibly share a meal.

Ralph liked baseball cards and photography. His reputation was that he was always willing to help others. He had held part-time jobs at the Brooks Canning Factory and Raintree Industries, a vocational rehabilitation service. He did odd jobs when he could find them, exchanging small labors for cigarette money. He also went into local bars, photographed people and attempted to sell them the prints.

Murder was not even a fleeting thought for Ralph that Valentine's Day. His dad owned two shotguns for hunting. One was an antique; both were locked up. Ralph never touched them. He hated guns. On New Year's Eve, Ralph Sr. liked to go out into the fields behind his house with his brother and some friends and fire the guns at midnight.

Ralph Jr. never went out with the other men. He hid in the house, terrified by the noise.

Nothing in his protected and predictable life could have prepared him for the aftermath of Wesley Crandall's murder. The routine investigation shattered his world.

On the day of the murder Ralph's mother told him to stay close. She would need him later. Having given Ralph these instructions, Janet left around 1:00 p.m. to pick up Ralph's pregnant sister, Loretta Cooper, and take her to her doctor's appointment. About 3:00 p.m., Janet stopped for groceries at the local Kroger store. She then drove Loretta to her home and returned to her own house about 5:00 p.m. Her drive home was not pleasant. In the blowing snow her windshield wipers stopped working.

Janet pulled into the driveway on the north side of the house and called for Ralph to come carry in the groceries. Ralph was still playing with his VCR but at his mother's call he left his cartoons and carried in the bags; with her severe asthma the task was difficult for her. He put the food away and then helped his mother start supper.

Wood-burning stoves heated both the house and the garage. Ralph's next task was to carry in wood. He could manage two to four sticks of wood per trip, but he carried in enough wood to last a week, filling the box and then piling it up along the wall.

Then he filled the box in the garage. Uncle Levi Jacobs had a tiny room partitioned off in the garage where he liked to sleep on weekends. A gas heater warmed the space but Levi was grateful to his nephew for bringing warmth to the work space in the garage.

Ralph ate a quiet supper of beef stew and biscuits with his parents. Uncle Levi was not invited. Janet did not like her husband's brother and preferred not to put herself out for him. She would bring him groceries if he asked in advance but she wouldn't make a special trip for him.

About 7:30 p.m., Levi asked Ralph to hike a few blocks to the North End Market to fetch some necessities for him. The store was close and the list simple: bread, milk, lunchmeat, and cigarettes. Ralph frequently ran errands for Levi, who was generous in supplying him with cigarette money. He returned home around 8:00 p.m., shook off the cold and settled in to watch television. He had tired of the entertainment and gone upstairs when his father received a bizarre phone call.

Jerry Johnson was a local man who had a warped sense of humor. He was fond of making prank phone calls that upset people, but the late-night call he made to the Jacobs's home was weird even for him. Johnson told Ralph's father that the police were at the Bamboo, a local tavern, looking for

Ralph Jr. Police were claiming that Ralph and another guy had killed someone.

Ralph Sr. thought the call was a joke but he did not laugh. "That stupid boy," he said, referring to Johnson. Killed somebody? Ralph Jr. wouldn't even accompany his dad on a hunting trip for fear he might have to kill a rabbit.

"And that's when Jim Stephens and them other cops started showing their weight down there at the door," Janet said. Ralph had been in bed when his father hollered for him to come down. He wore no shirt or shoes but pulled on his pants as he climbed down the stairs. Janet said, "That's when Stephens pushed the door open, about knocked me down and got rough with Ralph Jr. for no reason and Ralph, he said he'd go willingly with them to answer their questions."

Officers followed him upstairs and stayed with him while he dressed.

Ralph Jacobs stood five feet, six inches tall and weighed 160 pounds. He had brown hair and blue eyes and had an eerie resemblance to Douglas Percy. Jacobs told the officers he had been home all day but offered to go with them voluntarily.

He was taken directly to the office of Detective Captain Jim Stephens of the New Castle police force. Indiana State Police Investigator Ed Davis was also present. Given an Interrogation-Advice of Rights form, Jacobs claimed he could read it himself. He signed a waiver of his Miranda rights.

During a thirty-minute interview that was not taped, Jacobs told Stephens and Davis that he had never met Crandall and knew nothing about his murder. No formal statement was taken and Jacobs was returned to his home.

The following evening, officers returned to the Jacobs home. Janet answered and again, Jacobs voluntarily went to police headquarters to be questioned. The Rights and Waiver of Rights forms were again duly signed and witnessed.

Stephens would later report that he read the documents to Jacobs, who also read them himself.

A ten-minute interview was conducted but not taped. This was followed by a seven-minute taped interview in which Jacobs denied any knowledge of the crime committed at Crandall's residence the evening before. On the tape, Jacobs stated that he had read and understood his Miranda rights and had chosen to sign a waiver of those rights. He denied knowing Crandall or ever having visited Crandall's residence.

Following this interview was another conversation that was not taped in which Jacobs was informed that there were witnesses who placed him at the scene of the murder. Stephens, stepping out for a break, encountered Ralph Jacobs Sr. The elder Jacobs, terminally ill with a heart condition, had made the trip to the station to see about his son.

Upon questioning Mr. Jacobs, Stephens learned that, although the father believed his son had been home at the time of the murder, watching television, he had not actually seen him between 4:00 p.m. and 8:00 p.m. Stephens shouted at the sick man, telling him that his son was a liar.

Stephens returned to the interview room to inform Jacobs that he was a fucking liar who had no alibi. Also confronted with Gladys Case's statements, Jacobs began to admit that on occasions he had been to Crandall's apartment house. He said he had photographed Crandall's pit bulls for him.

Jacobs offered a new version of his story. He met his friend Charlie Alcorn, and together they went to Crandall's house. Alcorn had a shotgun in his old beat-up truck parked at the Bamboo. He retrieved this gun and he took it along, telling Ralph he had some business to settle with Crandall. Ralph said he thought Alcorn was going to trade the shotgun for some dope.

They entered the house without knocking. Jacobs said that Alcorn and Crandall argued over some money that Crandall supposedly owed to Alcorn. When Crandall refused to hand over the money, Alcorn kicked him behind the knees, knocked him down, and ran to get a pillow. Alcorn placed a pillow over Crandall's head, ordered Crandall to hold it, and shot him through the pillow.

"Did he say anything before he was shot?" Stephens asked.

"Yes, but I couldn't understand him because it was muffled from the pillow being over his head," Ralph replied.

After the shooting, Ralph said he "just waited while Charlie went upstairs and got the pot."

Alcorn left with a white plastic bag supposedly holding marijuana. Jacobs said that after they left, Alcorn gave him five dollars for cigarettes.

Everyone took a break and then investigators taped Jacobs repeating this story. They related that Jacobs was cooperative, did not seem nervous and asked for no favors. Jacobs was asked to remain at police headquarters until Alcorn was arrested so that he could identify him. Jacobs agreed to do so. Alcorn was arrested within hours and identified by Jacobs.

Stephens said the investigators gathered to discuss Ralph's statement and possible charges against him. They elected to release him "awaiting further developments in the case."

Police again returned Jacobs to his home.

CHAPTER 5—A GUILTY LOOKING GUY

At 11:00 p.m. on February 15, 1991, Charles Alcorn was picked up and advised of his rights, using the standard Interrogation-Advice of Rights form. He appeared nervous and was physically shaking as he read and signed the form.

Stephens began talking about Junior Crandall. Alcorn told Stephens that Crandall was a good friend, and he couldn't believe someone would do something like that to him. He said he had not seen Crandall lately. But when Stephens told him, "I have a confession from a person who said that you were with him when you shot Junior and killed him," Alcorn's nervousness evaporated.

"Jim, you got the wrong person," Alcorn protested. "I didn't do this to Junior, he was my friend."

Stephens shook his head. "Based on the information I have I'm going to have to hold you on a preliminary charge of murder."

Alcorn responded, "Then I don't have anything else to say except I want a lawyer" Nothing else was said to Alcorn. Police contacted Malcolm Edwards, the Henry County Prosecutor, and obtained a warrant to search the home of Charles Alcorn. In their search of the house, police officers recovered several ounces of marijuana from the bedroom. It was tagged and marked for evidence.

But by 4:00 p.m. the next day, February 16, it became clear that Alcorn had an alibi for the time of the slaying. A man named Charles Gregory confirmed that Alcorn could not have been at the murder scene.

Also, Mark Winchester finally came forward after several days, saying that he had been afraid to get involved and also had heard that the killer had already been arrested. Winchester identified the second man as thirty-two-year-old "Smitty," Christopher C. Smith. He said he was 90–95 percent certain that Smitty was one of the men he saw entering Crandall's apartment the evening of February 14. He described Smitty as a crippled man with a big leg.

Winchester offered other details. Smitty worked for Mr. Razor who took care of the vending machines on the south end of town. Winchester offered his statement but was not shown any photographs. Law enforcement had no pictures of Christopher Smith.

Stephens now knew that there were two people involved and that if Charlie Alcorn was in fact, not the shooter, he could be innocent. Officers invited Ralph Jacobs down for another chat.

Police came to pick Ralph up and question him four times. "Next thing they took him up and held him," his mother said. Police arrived on the evening of the 17th. "They had guns pulled and everything," Janet said. She stood by, helpless and horrified. "Stephens went upstairs and handcuffed my son on the way down, like, just about knocking him down, down the stairs, making him fall, handcuffing him."

Questions came up about Chris Smith, but Janet Jacobs had never heard of him. "I'd never met the guy until after it, the court started," she said.

Having advised him of his rights, Stephens asked Ralph who his best friend was. "Wayne Daniels," Ralph replied. "He's a fella lives in an apartment over by the courthouse."

Officers picked up Wayne Daniels. "Mr. Daniels appeared to have no trouble answering our questions," Stephens reported. "Nothing could be detected to cause us to form an opinion that he might be involved."

Ralph had mentioned that he wanted to talk to Wayne, so after he had been questioned, investigators allowed the two men to converse privately. Fifteen minutes later, Daniels emerged and said, "Ralph will talk to you now." When the officers returned, Wayne stayed in the room at Ralph's request.

Stephens explained to Ralph that they had questioned other people who gave Alcorn an alibi, and now believed they knew who was with Ralph at the time of the murder. "Ralph after some deliberation said that he had lied about Alcorn and that he was with a man named Smith," Stephens stated. Ralph did not know the man's first name; he only knew him as Smitty.

In a new, un-taped interview, this time with Daniels in the room, Ralph's story again changed. He had met "a guy" at 18th and Broad Streets. Ralph accompanied this guy to the residence of the victim. A shotgun was somehow obtained. The guy with Ralph and the victim argued over some money that the victim owed to the guy. During the fight, Ralph got on top of the victim and put a knee in his back. Then the guy, Smitty, shot the victim.

Investigators wanted more details. Ralph Jacobs tried again.

Asked to describe his companion, Ralph said, "About my size with dark hair and a mustache and he's crippled in his left leg."

The investigators said that wasn't much to go on. How had the murder occurred?

According to the investigative report: "Ralph said that he had gotten with Smith earlier and that Smith had asked him to go to Junior's with him. They walked south on 18th and just before they arrived Smith asked him to wait on the corner while he went someplace, telling him that he would be right back. Ralph said that Smith wasn't gone very long and when he returned, he was carrying a shotgun after which both walked to Junior Crandall's.

"They knocked at the door and was let in by Junior. After getting in they seen another man there talking to Junior. They waited until after he left and then Smitty and Junior got into an argument about some money that Junior owed Smith.

"They went into the kitchen, still arguing, and Smith knocked Junior down and he ran in and held his knee in Junior's back while Smith went into the other room and got the gun and a pillow from the bed.

"Smith gave the pillow to Junior to hold. Ralph said Junior held the pillow over his face and Smith was shouting for Junior to tell him where his money was."

Detective Stephens said, "I asked Ralph if Junior ever told and he said, 'I don't know. I couldn't understand what he was saying because of the pillow.'"

The report of Smith's testimony continued: "Then, after ordering Junior to hold the pillow, he, Smith, placed the shotgun against the pillow and shot Junior in the head." When the murder was done, Ralph waited while Smith went elsewhere in the apartment and returned with a white trash bag. Ralph said he did not actually see the marijuana, Smith told him what was in the bag.

In this version of the story, he went with Smith to Crandall's home to collect on a $1,000 drug debt. Also, during this interview, Ralph was able to supply details he could not have known if he were not there. He described the victim's billfold on the floor and said that there was a scale on the table.

Stephens reported, "After we finished talking, I asked Ralph to take a Voice Stress to show that he now was telling the truth and he agreed to this. All of his confession was given in the presence of Sergeant Cronk, Investigator Davis, Wayne Daniels, and myself.

"This same day Sergeant Cronk administered the Voice Stress and showed that Ralph was telling the truth about everything except the part about Junior holding the pillow.

Ralph said that he was the one who held the pillow, not Junior, and he held it until being told by Smith to step back and then Smith shot Junior in the head."

Ralph Jacobs claimed that these statements were true and that he would submit to a lie detector or Voice Stress Test to verify the truth of his statements. Another taped confession followed. Jacobs repeated his story. However, the tape of this confession was left in the machine and was inadvertently taped over the next day.

Beneath what appeared to be a façade of Jacobs's helpful cooperation, he was feeling tortured. Questioning continued for several hours on multiple days. Jacobs repeatedly asked for a lawyer and was told he didn't need one.

The fact of his innocence seemed irrelevant compared to the witnesses and tapes investigators held. Jacobs said, "I didn't think it mattered anymore."

Christopher C. "Smitty" Smith was arrested the next day. Following his arrest, Jacobs was also formally arrested. Wolfman and Smitty did not know each other. They had at times seen each other at a local tavern but were not acquainted. Yet each would claim that they were together on the night of February 14 in Crandall's apartment and that they were the killers. Neither man was able to say what happened to the murder weapon.

CHAPTER 6—A KILLER COMES FORTH

Thirty-three-year-old Christopher Columbus Smith walked some excruciating miles on the day that Junior Crandall died. Beside the cruel wind and finger-numbing temperature, Smith's steps were impeded by blowing snow, slick sidewalks, and his grossly swollen left leg. He claimed that the leg was a souvenir from an old auto accident and subsequent surgery.

According to his medical records, he also suffered from neurofibromatosis, a genetic disorder that causes tumors to grow on nerve tissue. His skin swelled with a number of erratic bumps. Neurofibromatosis was blamed for Chris's chronic memory loss and a malady known as elephantiasis or "elephant leg."

His face, head, and neck were dotted with old acne scars. Two upper front teeth were missing. He had curly dark-brown hair and blue eyes. He had tattoos on his arms. Except for his hair and eyes, at five feet, nine inches tall and weighing 174 pounds, Chris bore no physical resemblance to a murderer named Jerry Thompson.

Chris was considered retarded. He had attended school through the eleventh grade in special education classes. He was kicked out for hitting a teacher. "The defendant stated that the teacher referred to the students as 'sons of bitches,'" according to an investigative report.

The accused murderer could spell his name but no other words. He could recognize letters of the alphabet but not when they were combined into short words, and he recognized numbers only as single digits. He said that his best talent was electrical work and that he wanted to be a race car driver.

In the past, Chris had done seasonal work for the Morgan Packing Company, operating a forklift. He also earned a little income from sporadic farm labor.

The second of seven children, Chris raised four of his siblings, two of whom were labeled "slow learners." His father, Chris Smith Sr., had died of a heart attack in 1968 at age fifty-six. His mother, Ena Smith, succumbed to cancer in 1978, at age forty-three.

With both parents dead by the time he was nineteen, Chris assumed the tasks of parenting. Eventually the Welfare Department removed a brother and sister from his home. The memory of losing his siblings lingered like a hot and infected wound in Chris Smith's heart.

At the time of Crandall's murder, Chris was divorced. He married his first wife, Vicki Davis, in 1979. The marriage lasted about a year. There were no children.

In 1982, he married Bonnie Baker. During their four-year marriage there were two children. Each died at birth.

Chris did not marry again until 1990, when he wedded Nancy Ellis. Nancy found her husband suffocating. She said he would not let her go anywhere without him, not even to the store. On August 8, 1990, their son, Chris Lynn Smith, was born. When the marriage dissolved at the end of a year, Nancy took Chris's child and moved to Hagerstown, Indiana.

Pam Short became Chris's fourth wife on February 16, 1991, two days after Crandall's death. Since Chris was arrested the day after they wed, Pam divorced Chris in September of 1991. He had no further contact with her.

The day before the murder, February 13, Chris spent the day with his brother, twenty-eight-year-old Tracy Dean

Smith. The pair walked to the Stonegate apartments where Tracy's estranged wife, Tina A. Smith, lived in Apt. 26. They made the trek only to discover that Tina had taken off with her mother. Chris and Tracy waited for a while, watching television. Eventually they gave up and went back to Chris's house.

On the night before the murder, Chris went to the Twilight, a tavern on 19th Street, and drank beer with Tracy and a man about thirty years old named Jerry. The brothers did not know Jerry's last name or where he lived, only that he was a local man who survived on Social Security benefits.

While they were there drinking, Chris got into a fight with a relative, Terry Alton. Smith claimed that Terry's brother had molested his niece. The people at the bar broke up the tussle and no one was hurt. Chris, Tracy, and Jerry stayed until the tavern closed at 1:00 a.m. All three men returned to Chris's house, deeply drunk.

Tracy said that Chris was still angry. After Tracy fell into a drunken sleep, Chris got up and fired a 20 gauge shotgun out the front door. He quickly realized that not everyone would see the humor in his prank so he hid the gun up in the ceiling tiles of the front room in case the police came around asking questions.

The brothers awakened on the morning of February 14 at approximately 8:00 a.m. Their bar buddy, Jerry, was gone. About 10:00 a.m. they walked back to Stonegate. Tina was still missing in action. Hoping for the arrival of a check in the mail, Chris and Tracy waited around for the mailman but no check arrived. They then decided to walk over to visit their sister, Wyona Alton.

Wyona lived in New Castle at 2326 Grand, Apt. F-1. Chris was close with his sister and he enjoyed playing with his niece and nephew, Rebecca, age nine, and five-year-old William. They watched TV and all ate dinner together around 5:45. Chris left about 6:30 after watching an episode of *Full House*.

The walk home was about fifteen minutes. After he got there a message came over his police scanner, reporting some action going on in the 1200 block of 18th Street. Chris Smith and an acquaintance Robbie Barkley wandered over to see what had happened. People were saying there had been a murder, a man shot to death in his own home. Joe Wood, who lived in Crandall's block, filled the two in on what he knew but Smith said he did not know Wesley Crandall.

He returned home at 7:30 and ran into his landlord, Arthur J. Razor. Chris helped Razor fill seven Pepsi machines on "I" Street, around the corner from his house. He said the task took about fifteen minutes.

At 8:00 p.m., Chris went to the Twilight and stayed, again drinking beer until the tavern closed at 1:00 a.m.

Tracy went back to Stonegate and did not see Chris again until Sunday, February 17. Tracy and his wife, Tina, had spent the night at Wyona's house.

Chris arrived at his sister's residence looking for a bicycle he'd stored in her garage. He told Tracy he'd been to Kentucky doing a little work for Jim Gregory on his farm. Chris stayed at his sister's house for about half an hour and then took off on the bike.

The next day Jim Gregory came to Wyona's apartment and asked, "Is it true?" Tracy didn't know what the man was talking about but Gregory said, "Chris was arrested."

***

Christopher Smith was a wanted man in New Castle. Having heard witnesses pinpoint Smith as the shooter, Investigator Ernie Crabtree went immediately to the home of Smith's close friend Jack Ford. He expected that Smith would be there hanging out with his buddy, but Ford told the officer that Smith had gone to Kentucky.

It turned out that Smith was not hard to find. Within two hours of Jacobs's confession, Smith called the police station. "I heard you were looking for me?"

He said he had returned from Kentucky and spoken with Ford. A car was sent to pick him up. He was offered a standard Interrogation-Advice of Rights form. Stephens's report read, "Mr. Smith stated that he did not read well enough even though he had gone all the way through school lacking two weeks graduating. I had placed the date and time at the top of the page, which is standard procedure and I asked Smith if he could tell me the date and time. Smith looked and had no trouble reading this."

As for his rights, Stephens said, "I then asked him if he completely understood them and he said that he did, further I asked if he had any questions about his rights or the use of an attorney. Mr. Smith said he understood his rights and he had done nothing and was willing to talk."

Smith told the investigators that he did not know Junior Crandall and had never been to his home. Stephens said, "I then explained to Mr. Smith that there was a witness who had seen him and his friend there leaving the house together."

Smith again tried to deny being there but Stephens told him, "She lived across the street and she was going to her car and observed you and your friend leaving." She even knew Smitty's friend's nickname. "You remember seeing her, don't you?"

Smith started to answer and then said, "Oh. Yes, I have been there. I use to visit a girl who lived upstairs back last year."

"Chris, what have you got to hide?" Stephens prodded. "Because I know that you were there the day of the murder."

Then Chris said, "You're right. I forgot I was there about 2:00 o'clock with Wolfman."

Stephens related that he asked what Wolfman's name was and Chris responded that he did not know. "Does the name Ralph Jacobs sound familiar?" Stephens asked.

"Ralph does but not the other."

Continuing his report of the investigation, Stephens said, "I asked Smith to explain what it was they were doing there and he said that they had gone to Junior's to trade a gun for some pot but Junior didn't want the gun. I asked Chris if Junior owed him money, or did he owe Junior any money, and he said no to both questions. I asked him if he had ever bought pot from Junior before and he said yes, several times.

"I then explained that the lady across the street had seen them leaving carrying something and he said yes, we were carrying pot. I asked him to describe to me what they were carrying the pot in. He said a white like bag, sandwich or trash bag, whatever you want to call it. I asked him how much marijuana they left with and he said about $3,000 worth. I asked him to tell me about how much pot that would be and he said about a pound and a half."

Stephens' questioning unearthed more damning evidence. "Further, that he had taken the pot to Kentucky to a guy named Bill who was to sell the pot on consignment for him. Further, that he had gone to Kentucky with a man named James Gregory who he said that he worked for on his farm in Kentucky. I then asked Chris if he would give me a statement about this. He said he would.

"After taking the above information on tape I asked Chris how it was that they went there to trade a gun for pot but when they left, they left with $3,000 in pot and the gun. Smith first said that Junior gave it to him but I told him that Ralph had already given a statement about what happened, and then Smith said okay, I'll tell you what happened.

"Smith said that they had gone there to trade the gun but he got into it with Junior, and Ralph shot Junior in the head while he held the pillow over Junior's head.

"I then explained to Chris that Ralph had given a totally different story and had backed up his story with a Voice Stress Test and had passed it."

Three hours after he was brought to the police station, Christopher Smith changed his story. He and Ralph had gone to Junior's house. They knocked on the door and when they entered, Junior put his pit bulls in an adjoining room. They began to talk about money.

Stephens said, "I asked Chris to explain why Junior owed him money and he said because we were in the dope business together and Junior had promised to pay him a thousand dollars from the sale of the dope, because they were using his apartment for the dope drop. He said two men driving a blue '67 Chevy had dropped off three pounds two weeks earlier and he was to be paid from the sale of some other dope and Junior was going to keep all that he made from these three pounds, but after getting there Junior refused to pay him any money and they argued about this and he knocked Junior to the floor and Wolfman jumped on his back and held him while he went to the other room and returned with a pillow.

"This was placed over Junior's head by Wolfman and he stuck the shotgun against Junior's head and he told Wolfman to move back then he shot Junior in the head." The narrative continued, Smith describing himself and Wolfman leaving Junior's house and going north on 18th. "He was carrying the gun with the stock under his arm so as to hide it and Ralph was carrying the white trash bag."

***

Chris Smith's later description of the process was less formulaic.

When Jim Stephens and Kim Cronk questioned Chris, he told the investigators that he knew nothing about the murder. But Stephens told him again that a witness put him at the scene of the shooting. Stephens made Chris nervous, tapping his pencil on the desk, turning a tape recorder on and off. Chris still insisted he knew nothing and was asked to sign permission for police to search his residence. Chris said, "I let them go search my place 'cause I didn't have nothin' to hide."

But the questioning continued. Stephens told Chris that a witness named Ralph Jacobs had already confessed that he was with him on the scene. Jacobs said that he went into the bedroom, got a pillow, put it over Junior Crandall's head and then Chris shot him.

Chris tried to argue that he had been at his sister's house at the time of the murder but Jim Stephens said he was lying, that there were witnesses who put him on the scene, pulling the trigger that slammed a coffin lid on Wesley Crandall's life.

Winchester had recognized him. Stephens had provided Winchester with a photo array consisting of twelve pictures. Winchester selected number eight, Christopher "Smitty" Smith. In short, Christopher Smith was the person Gladys Case had described as carrying what appeared to be a gun in a concealed manner.

Chris insisted he was not acquainted with Crandall, and certainly had not been at his home that day. He had been at his sister's house at the time Crandall was killed, or he was at home in his own apartment.

His arguments were pointless. There were multiple witnesses. Cornered, Chris confessed.

In a taped statement Chris told Detective Stephens that he and Junior Crandall got into an argument. He knocked Crandall down and then Ralph Jacobs held him while he went to get a pillow. Then Ralph held the pillow over Crandall's head while Chris shot him. He said his motive was that Crandall owed him money, about a thousand dollars. He said that Crandall owed him the money because he and Junior were partners in the sale of marijuana. He said that Crandall bought the dope, and it was dropped off at Smith's place and later delivered to Crandall.

Chris said, "Me and Ralph Jacob went there and I'm the one who pulled the trigger." He claimed that he saw Crandall's wallet on the table, took about $300 from it, and left it lying on the floor. He said he also carried away about a pound and a half of pot in a white garbage bag.

What happened to the murder weapon? Chris had no idea.

Chris's brother, Tracy, doubted Chris could be the killer. Chris had never been to Junior Crandall's house and did not know the man, Tracy said. Nor did Tracy. Tracy only knew Ralph Jacobs as the "Wolfman" who took pictures. Tracy's wife was teed off at the Wolfman because he promised her some pictures of her brother-in-law's race car, but he never delivered them.

Plus, Tracy argued, they never found the murder weapon. The newspaper said Crandall was killed with a 12 gauge. It could not have been Chris's. It was the wrong kind of shotgun.

Tracy didn't believe Chris was a killer but he did think his brother was a liar. He simply could not swallow the story that Chris had married a fourth wife in Kentucky. "He's not got no wife down there in Kentucky," Tracy insisted, "and sometimes he lies about all of us. He lies about his legs and everything." Everything but murder.

Anna Stewart questioned Smith's guilt too. Crandall knew Smith and did not trust him. Also, he was cautious about his business. He did not sell joints and hadn't for a long time. Anna said, "He would only do a large volume at a time but what I would consider a large volume you know he would sell quarters, ounces, pounds, things like that."

Stewart stated that Crandall would never have sold to either Jacobs or Smith. She said, "Junior's ex-girlfriend, Sandy, told me that Christopher Smith had came over there one time and Junior got upset about it and told her that if he ever came back, she was not to let him in."

Christopher Smith had danced a few do-si-dos with the law. In 1976, he was arrested for leaving the scene of a property damage accident. The city court took no action. In 1983, his offense was public intoxication. The court withheld judgment. Three years later, he was again intoxicated and disorderly, and he resisted arrest. He was fined ten dollars plus court costs.

In 1989, Smith was sentenced to thirty days in the county jail for public intoxication. He also admitted that he had once been arrested for petty theft in Tennessee, but the charges were dismissed.

Chris's ability to lie soon came under examination. On March 15, 1991, he faced a polygraph test. He understood that the test was supposed to reveal the truth of the Crandall matter. If Chris told the truth, if he told them that he had killed no one, then surely, he would be released? He had not seen his infant son in a month.

Chris was taken from the Henry County Jail and delivered to the State Police post in Connersville, Indiana. There he was met by H.R. Chambers, Laboratory Division, Indiana State Police, who subjected him to a polygraph test. Ed Davis, detective for the Indiana State Police, gave the polygraphist background information on the Crandall murder. Then Chambers was ready to question Chris. Three tests followed, which included these relevant questions:

1. Do you intend to lie to me during this examination?
    No.
2. Have you told me the complete truth since we've been talking?
    Yes.
3. Do you know for sure who shot Junior?
    No.
4. Did you fire the shot that killed Junior?
    No.
5. Were you telling the truth in your statement when you said you shot Junior?
    No.

6. Are you telling the truth when you deny shooting Junior?

Yes.

After the tests, Chambers reported his conclusion. "The test records of Mr. Chris Smith did contain specific reactions to Question #3 relating to knowledge and cannot be cleared as having told the complete truth during his examination."

CHAPTER 7—MAKING OF A KILLER

By the first of the week, police announced that they had a break in their investigation of the Thursday night, February 14th shooting. The front page of New Castle's *Courier-Times* daily newspaper reported that two local men, Jacobs and Smith, had been arrested and charged with Crandall's murder. The message was echoed in the *Indianapolis Star*.

Thompson was elated over the arrests of Wolfman and Smitty. He'd gotten away with murder. He had killed a man and was richer for the effort. He'd scored a fortune in marijuana and had some new guns.

Thompson wasted no time. He destroyed some of the stolen guns and sold others. He used one of them as payment for some used furniture. The best ones were held in reserve to be used in future murders.

All he needed to do was grind the serial numbers off the weapons and then he had the power to walk around and do as he pleased to whomever he pleased. Jerry Thompson was a beast on the prowl.

***

Americans have a fascination with crime shows. Viewers dedicate prime-time hours to both true and fictional accounts of murder. We root for the great crime solvers and talk about them as if they were our cousins. Whether analyzing clues on *48 Hours*, or second-guessing the actors on *NCIS*, we want to know what sort of person would kill another. More importantly, we want to know why.

What these shows gift us with is the "why?"—knowledge we can never have in real life. Night after night the producers ensure that we gain full answers in an hour's time. Television offers viewers a vicarious sense of security.

It's like solving the puzzle makes us feel safer. And since we've seen the episode, we will never park on the wrong level of a garage at night. We will be aware of painted warnings and strange noises and not stumble unawares onto a drug deal. We will note the odd family member who seems overly concerned with our property and wealth.

But people are complicated and TV answers don't fit real life. When historians try to evaluate what made Adolph Hitler a monster, they examine all the factors that converged to shape him: family history, personality, life events, economics, politics, and world events.

In the same way, Jerry Thompson was not born into this world bearing the kind of rage that would enable him to turn a deadly weapon on another human being. He was shaped by hunger and want, pain and disappointment, terror and trauma. He was ignited and set ablaze by thousands of daily events that taught him he would have nothing in this life if he did not take it by force.

Jerry Kevin Thompson was born amid the celebration of St. Patrick's Day, March 17, 1961, the fifth child of Marvin and Sara Thompson. He was born in a hospital, the birth without trauma, and taken home by his mother a few days later. Dad was not there to welcome him. Dad was in jail—again. Jerry's elder siblings were twelve-year-old Tony, seven-year-old Steve, four-year-old Susan, and David, aged two.

New Castle, Indiana, the county seat of Henry County, was a city of approximately 20,000 people. It seemed like a decent place to rear a child. There were good schools and crime rates were low.

The community was predominantly white and most of its citizens were working-class people. Surrounded by agriculture, New Castle had been an industrial haven for decades. It was the birthplace of Wilbur Wright. Before the automotive industry, New Castle produced world renowned Krell-French pianos and Hoosier Kitchen cabinets.

In 1959, New Castle Chrysler High School became the home of the world's largest high school gymnasium, New Castle Fieldhouse. The Fieldhouse, with a seating capacity of 9,235, had a recessed court. Spectators strolled in at ground level, walked down to their seats, and had an aerial view of the gym floor.

The basketball court, which was still ranked number one by *USA Today* in 2004, nurtured Indiana University stars Kent Benson and Steve Alford, who went on to become College All-American and NBA players.

In the city's Baker Park loomed a Native American mound dating to approximately 2000 BP. The city tree, the Golden Raintree, was based on a legend of Johnny Appleseed. It was said that Johnny Appleseed carried one exotic seed in his pouch, and that he was looking for a place where the Golden Raintree could grow and flourish. He was said to have planted that seed somewhere in Henry County, and the finder of that tree would realize all their dreams.

In the midst of New Castle dreams was a nightmare, a private hell, and Jerry Thompson was born into that place of torture. Jerry's horror story is one that has become all too common in our culture. His rat-infested homes, usually one or two rooms, often had no plumbing, just an outhouse. Every three to six months, the family moved to another hovel. Sometimes they were evicted, other times the place was condemned, or Jerry's father, Marvin, was running from the law.

The events that would lead Jerry Thompson to become a killer began long before he was born. Neither of Jerry Thompson's parents came from a stable or nurturing family. Neither parent had any formal education, job training, or the type of family and community support that would prepare them for parenthood.

Jerry's mother, Sara Roe Thompson, was born in New Castle in 1930. Her father, William Roe, was a notorious alcoholic who was said to have escaped from a North Carolina prison. William disappeared before Sara was born, leaving her mother, Elizabeth Roe, to rear Sara and an older sister. Sara never met her dad until she was in her twenties.

Sara's mother, a Pentecostal preacher, later married Alonzo Lowe. A cruel man, Lowe physically beat Sara. He later went to prison for the sexual abuse of one of Sara's ten younger half-siblings. Sara fled the home at age seventeen. She had an eighth-grade education, having dropped out of school to go to work.

Sara did factory work at Firestone and RCA, but most of her life she worked second and third jobs. She cleaned houses, did laundry, and sold Avon and Tupperware products. No matter how hard she worked, she could not meet the needs of five growing children and a husband who drank up every penny.

The Thompson children often went to bed without eating. Their clothes were secondhand and ill fitting. Although Sara denied herself—for a long period of time, several years, Jerry said, she owned a single dress that she laundered each night to wear to work the next day—there was never enough money to cover the basics: food, clothes, bedding, school supplies, medical care, and personal hygiene.

Most of the family's food came from Sara's talent as a shoplifter. Sara taught her children early that if they wanted to eat, they must steal. She used them to glean food and other necessities from store shelves.

By the time Jerry was ten years old, Sara was disabled with rheumatoid arthritis and other health issues related to her extreme weight, which topped 400 pounds.

Jerry's father, Marvin Walter Thompson, had a sixth-grade education. He met Sara in 1949. They had their first child that year and married in 1951. A Kentucky native who moved to New Castle at age fourteen, Marvin had previously been married and had a son by that union, James Walter Thompson.

Sara claimed that what little money Marvin had, came from thefts and burglaries. His only employer was Dann Brothers Junkyard but Sara claimed he was "a safecracker and hog-thief." Locals nicknamed Marvin "Hoggy," and the rumor mill claimed that he not only stole pigs but brutally sodomized them.

Frequently jailed for illicit activities, Marvin's rap sheet comprised seventy-two offenses dating back to the 1950s. When Marvin was incarcerated, the family had a modicum of peace, but those breaths were uneasy and short-lived. Sara visited the jail, using the children to smuggle contraband to their dad. According to Jerry's sister, Susan, it was the Dann brothers who, "for some reason" continually stepped in to bail Marvin out of jail.

A raging alcoholic, Marvin provided virtually nothing toward the needs of his family. He offered his young children alcohol instead of food, teaching them to drink from an early age. He beat Sara frequently and without mercy. He abused and tormented his children as if their pain satisfied an addiction.

At a young age, Jerry saw his dad beat his mother so savagely that she stumbled into the bathroom and suffered a miscarriage, dropping a fetus into the toilet. Marvin disposed of the child with a flush of satisfaction saying, "I don't need another bastard anyhow."

He claimed that all of his children were bastards and that he could name their fathers. Having survived the beating and the miscarriage, Sara was forced to walk to the doctor to receive medical care.

Jerry's sister, Susan, said that Marvin Thompson, "was not a father. He used his kids for his own amusement."

Marvin's idea of entertainment was savagery. To amuse his friends, he'd have Jerry fight his brother, David. The winner would be allowed to eat that day. Since David was bigger and two years older, Jerry was easily beaten down.

Marvin would also throw some money or whatever food the family had into the middle of the floor and force them to fight for it. Jerry, youngest and smallest in the family, usually lost. Marvin often beat Jerry, either because he wasn't "tough enough" or for no reason at all, stuffing a sock in his mouth so he could not cry out as he lashed him with a belt.

One can only conjecture about events in Marvin's life that drove him to torture his own family. Yet his children avowed that his wrath was swift and unpredictable and that his cruelty could have come straight out of a horror movie.

Marvin Thompson's abuse was also sexual. He resented his youngest son for being a crybaby and a sissy. Once he caught Jerry taking a bath. He laughed, grabbing and fiercely squeezing the boy's testicles. "You think you're a man?" he mocked.

At ages six and eight, Jerry and David were taken by their father on a rare excursion to the park. Marvin conned his wife out of money for the outing but he left the boys to fend for themselves while he went out whoring and drinking with the cash. Sometime after dark the boys walked home alone.

A couple of years later Marvin again took the boys to the park. This time he returned with a woman and was too drunk to drive. Ten-year-old David had to drive them home.

Jerry once asked why his dad gave money to David, but never gave him any. "Because he's a cocksman and you're a cocksucker," his dad replied.

Sister Susan, four years older than Jerry, began babysitting her brothers at age ten. She took care of them the way she'd been taught, hitting them with her hands and fists. Susan often went out at night to track down her dad at local bars. When he was drunk enough, she would steal money from him to buy food.

By middle school, Jerry and David found themselves frequently at home alone. They began to skip school together. Chronic truancy trounced Jerry's grades and he repeated seventh grade twice. Jerry said he wanted to be in sports but those activities cost money. He had to settle for building his reputation as the neighborhood's toughest kid.

Having learned at a young age to steal in order to eat, Jerry became a proficient thief but could find no way to please his father. Despite the abuse and verbal humiliation, Jerry adored Marvin and he yearned for his dad's love and respect. The troubled child of a troubled man took to the streets to create some havoc of his own.

Soon Jerry was getting into trouble with the law. In his twelfth year, Jerry was arrested four times for vandalism, truancy, runaway, and being incorrigible. There was no investigation of Jerry's home and parents. He received no counseling or professional assistance. His arrests resulted in "Informal Adjustment;" a report was written but no action was taken. He was sent back into his tragic home environment.

The four older children each moved out as soon as they turned sixteen years of age. Susan at age sixteen, pregnant with her first child, might have stayed, but when her father sexually assaulted her, she ran for her own safety. This left Jerry, age twelve, and fourteen-year-old David to absorb their father's need for savagery. It seemed that Marvin had always taken his greatest delight in brutalizing Jerry, youngest and weakest of the tribe.

By age thirteen Jerry was smoking marijuana and damaging property. Arrested and adjudicated a delinquent minor, he was ordered to make restitution for petty crimes that included criminal mischief and shoplifting. At sixteen, he was charged with battery and at last taken from the home and placed with his older brother, Steve. As Jerry's guardian, Steve had little to offer. Steve had been to Boys' School, had a rap sheet, and was using and selling drugs.

Jerry dropped out of school his junior year. He later completed his GED at Chrysler High School.

He joined the National Guard a few months after his seventeenth birthday. His new military career lasted almost three months. He was discharged after he was injured by some military equipment. Numerous bones were broken in Thompson's hand when it was crushed by a tank track weighing approximately 800 pounds.

No longer of any use to the military, Jerry found himself with no home to go to. He drifted from one criminal element to the next. He abused drugs and alcohol.

A month later, Jerry stole a vehicle. He was living with his brother David at the time. Jerry, accompanied by an adult male, and two juvenile females stole a car and drove it to Chicago. They were apprehended and Jerry Thompson was sentenced to Boys' School on November 27, 1978. He was released on April 3, 1979, weeks after his eighteenth birthday.

At age eighteen, now a legal adult, Thompson left the structure of Boys' School and returned to the chaos of aimless wandering. That year he was arrested for driving without a license, for illegal consumption and disorderly conduct, and for burglary. He would spend nine of his next eleven years of life incarcerated for burglary, theft, auto theft, rape, child molestation, and escape.

Thompson's adult height was six feet, five inches tall. Towering over most other men and having fought his whole life, he readily developed a reputation as a predator in prison. Stories told by Douglas Percy and also other prison inmates depict Thompson as surviving well behind bars.

His body was blanketed neck to toes with tattoos, most prominent of which advertised his dedication to racial hatred and white supremacy. Any man who wore dark skin was automatically Thompson's avowed enemy. Unwilling to bow to the desires of any man of color, Thompson started fights, even if the provocation was no more than a look that was not submissive enough.

One thing is certain: Thompson did exert authority over other prisoners. On more than one occasion, when the inmates were creating problems, authorities claim it was Thompson who ordered his fellow prisoners to calm down and helped bring an incident under control.

When Thompson was again paroled, he was determined he would not return to jail. With limited work experience and a rap sheet, he was unlikely to find a good job. But early training had taught him that there were other ways to get money and drugs. And he knew how to take what he wanted.

CHAPTER 8—A
DOUBLE HOMICIDE

The Thursday evening murder of Wesley Crandall was solved by Sunday night. Both Ralph Jacobs Jr. and Christopher Smith were taken into custody. On the following Thursday, February 21, 1991, both men told Judge Thomas McNichols they were not guilty. During the proceedings, Smith said he did not commit the crime, "but I am being accused of it."

Despite the pleas of both men, the charges stood. Smith's trial was set for Tuesday, May 21, and Jacobs's trial for Tuesday, May 28.

Though he had committed no crime and knew nothing about the murder, Jacobs went into court and confessed, agreeing that he held Crandall down and placed a pillow over his head while Smith, the triggerman, shot him.

Because of Jacobs's confession the State dismissed the higher felony charge, Aiding in Commission of Offense of a Murder, and charged Jacobs with a Class C Felony Battery.

The Class C Felony Battery charge, to which Ralph Jacobs pled guilty, was defined by the Indiana Criminal Code as "knowingly or intentionally touching another person in a rude, insolent, or angry manner by means of a deadly weapon or resulting in serious bodily injury to another person." Indiana Criminal Code I.C. 35-42-1 (a) (3) stated, "The crime is punishable by a fixed term of imprisonment of four (4) years, to which up to four (4) years could be added for aggravating circumstances (such as prior criminal record and nature and circumstances of the crime) and from which up to two (2) years could be subtracted for mitigating circumstances (such as lack of any significant criminal record and diminished mental capacity.)"

Felony Battery means a deliberate and intentional attack that causes a victim physical injury or pain. Battery charges are ranked A, B, C, or D, with A being the most serious. A charge of Class C Felony Battery in Indiana means that the attacker caused "serious bodily injury" to the victim and/or that a deadly weapon was used in the commission of the crime. A deadly weapon can be defined as not only a traditional weapon of death, such as a firearm or knife, but also an animal or object, in this case, a pillow.

Indiana legislature allowed the judge to order a fixed term of imprisonment from the range allowed by law. The judge could also pass an advisory sentence, somewhere between the minimum and maximum, as advised by the legislature. Penalties for Class C Felony Battery were a prison term of four to eight years with an advisory judgment of four years. A fine of up to $10,000 could also be leveled at the judge's discretion.

Simply put, the judge was free to sentence Jacobs to imprisonment of any fixed term of between two and eight years, after giving due consideration to all aggravating and mitigating circumstances that might exist.

Prosecutor Malcolm K. Edwards, Ralph Jacobs Jr., and his attorney, Randall Sorrell, signed the agreement on October 15, 1991. The agreement was that Jacobs would plead guilty to Battery, a Class C Felony. In regard to sentencing, the agreement stated:

> "That defendant shall be sentenced to the Indiana Department of Correction for a period of eight years executed. That defendant shall give to investigators a complete statement, satisfactory to the State, about his involvement in and knowledge of events

surrounding the death of Wesley Crandall Jr. on February 14, 1991.

"The defendant shall testify truthfully about said events...

"The defendant additionally acknowledges satisfaction with defense counsel's representation and competency exhibited in this matter, and further acknowledges belief that this agreement is in the best interest of the defendant."

Unable to either read the two-page agreement or understand his attorney's explanation, Ralph Jacobs signed the paper because that was what he was told to do. Sentencing was set for January 23, 1992.

When interviewed by the probation department, Wesley Crandall's sister, Judy Steinbacher, opposed the plea agreement. "She advised that in a way she disagrees with the sentence recommendation due to the fact that he is pleading to only a Battery, when in fact, Junior was killed." While understanding that Jacobs's involvement was minimal compared to Chris Smith's, "She did state that she would want to be notified if the defendant would seek a sentence modification."

Jacobs's signature on the plea agreement would define him for the remainder of his life as a criminal. When Jacobs was sentenced in Henry Superior Court No. 1 on January 23, 1992, he had spent most of a year in jail. He stood before Judge Thomas R. McNichols; his heart so bruised he could barely breathe. Ralph Sr. had died on December 5, 1991, while Ralph was in custody for a crime he could not have committed.

The Court said that although Jacobs's previous criminal record showed only a couple of misdemeanors, "There appears to the Court to be a substantial risk that the defendant will commit another crime." It was also stated that Jacobs's actions with another led to a death and these were an aggravating circumstance. The Court described Jacobs as "of bad character but of basically good physical condition." The legal documents described him as a follower who could easily be led to participate in another wrongful death.

Thirty-one-year-old Ralph's prior criminal record declared two charges. On April 3, 1980, he was charged with Conversion, a Class A Misdemeanor, in the Henry County Court. He was fined ten dollars plus court costs. He was also sentenced to ten days in the Henry County Jail, but that was suspended.

Two years later, on August 2, 1982, Ralph was charged with Criminal Trespass, a Class A Misdemeanor and Criminal Mischief, a Class B Misdemeanor. His six-month sentence to the Indiana State Farm was suspended on good behavior. No fine or cost was assessed.

It is doubtful that Ralph understood the charges against him. He certainly could not have argued for himself the aggravating and mitigating circumstances. During the investigation, no one took a deposition from his family beyond Stephens asking his father if he'd seen him at home that day. Along with his attorney, Randall V. Sorrell, he signed the deal.

Wesley Crandall's family had originally agreed with the plea agreement, but as the day of sentencing approached, they opposed Jacobs's right to seek a modification of his sentence and wanted him to spend more time in prison than was allowed by the Battery charge. The Court said there were no mitigating circumstances. There were no factors that would influence the Court to consider a diminished sentence. Jacobs's limited mental capacity was not given consideration.

Judge McNichols sentenced Jacobs to the maximum term, eight years in prison. He would be given credit for the 341 days he had already spent in jail.

On October 15, 1991, Jacobs entered his guilty plea. He was declared indigent, a person so needy that he lacked the necessities of life. This excused him from paying court costs. But as he faced years of prison, Ralph Jacobs found himself stripped of more than physical needs. He'd had no opportunity to say goodbye to his father. If his mother now called for more wood or help with groceries, who would come? There would be no more long walks, no hot cups of coffee at the truck stop. Ralph knew he was being robbed of eight years of his life; he just wasn't sure how it had happened.

CHAPTER 9—A "LEGALLY RIGHT" DECISION

Once Jacobs had been dispatched, the Henry County Prosecutor and the Court turned their attention to the gunman, Christopher Smith. Confession in hand, Stephens delivered his evidence to Prosecutor Malcolm K. Edwards, who charged Smith with Murder, a Felony in the State of Indiana. Filed under I.C. 35-42-1-1, the charge read, "On or about February 14, 1991, you Christopher C. Smith did knowingly kill Wesley A. Crandall Jr., another human being by shooting at or against the body of Wesley Crandall Jr., with a gun and thereby inflicting a mortal wound upon said Wesley Crandall Jr., causing Wesley Crandall Jr. to die. All of that being contrary to and against the Indiana law."

The Court asked Chris Smith if he understood, if he knew what it all meant. Smith said yes, he did. Did he feel then that his plea of Guilty was his own free and voluntary act? Smith told the Court yes, it was.

For a killer, he did not appear to be a vicious individual. Small in stature, confused and bewildered, Smith was terrified to silence in the courtroom. Courtroom observers talked about him like he was an animal in a cage.

The Court had him scheduled for a psychiatric evaluation.

In April, 1991, two months after the murder, Christopher Smith came under the scrutiny of Thomas McConnell, MD. The psychiatrist evaluated Smith and reported his results of that examination to Judge McNichols.

"Chris Smith is a thirty-two-year-old white male, who comes into my office today dressed in an orange jail jumpsuit. He has a cross around his neck, which he states he made out of 'sock laces' woven together. He states he made this 'in jail because there is not much to do.' He has long, curly brown hair with a mustache and goatee. He has two missing upper front teeth and old facial, neck, and head acne scars. His left leg is grossly swollen, which according to him is secondary to a past automobile accident and subsequent surgery. His overall mood was pleasant and his facial affect was full range and appropriate to the content. Thought process was logical and clear and there was no past history of hallucinations. He is oriented as to time, place and person and demonstrated good immediate, recent, and remote memory. He is probably of below average intelligence as he is unable to read or write. Insight was considered fairly good and no serious defects in judgment were noted. The patient states that he was arrested 'because they said I did a murder, and I didn't do it. They got me arrested on another guy's word.' He states that this was 'supposed to have happened' on February 14, 1991. He says he was arrested on February 18, 1991, and he is currently in jail in New Castle, Indiana.

"The past family, personal, and social history reveals that both parents are deceased. Father died at age fifty-six of a heart attack and mother at age forty-three of cancer. The patient is the next to the oldest of a total of seven siblings. Two of these he states were 'slow learners.' These children are all still living. There is no history of mental illness, suicide, or known alcohol problems in the related family. He states about his family, 'I raised four of my brothers and sisters.' He states that he got to the eleventh grade in special education classes. He was first married from 1982 to 1986 and there were three children who are now deceased. He has one living child, a son, age eighteen months by a second union. (I am not certain but I do not believe he is married at this time.) He admits to being arrested three times, two of which were for public intoxication. He states that he drank daily and heavily following the divorce from his first wife but states that he has had nothing to drink since he met his second wife. He has never worked successfully in gainful employment. When asked what the most important thing to him in his life was, he stated, 'My son.' (Tears in his eyes.)"

The doctor's report was clear and factual, but it gave little credence to who Christopher Smith was as a person and how the legal proceedings affected him. Incarceration meant more to Chris Smith than loss of freedom. It meant he could not see his only living child. Little Chris was now in the custody of his estranged wife.

The report concluded: "With the history noted above and the mental status examination, which I did today, my opinion is that this client does not suffer from any psychopathology other than Mild Mental Retardation. Psychological testing would be necessary to determine the exact IQ. There may be a legitimately past medical history for the diagnosis of alcoholism.

"I feel that Christopher Smith is capable of aiding his attorney in his own defense and does understand the charges brought against him. I feel that he was probably sane at the time of the alleged offense."

Smith's background was summed up in a presentencing report, which stated that he was in fair health. "Physically, the defendant has several large bumps that appear on the surface of his skin. The defendant stated that the bumps started appearing after he was involved in an automobile accident. At this time, it is undetermined if there is a direct correlation of the defendant's accident and the appearance of the skin bumps. He was coherent in his thought processes and was oriented to time and space."

Having survived the normal childhood diseases, Smith claimed that later in life he suffered from a sickness that kept him from sleeping at night, but he had recovered. "He stated that approximately twelve years ago, he sustained injuries as a result of a race car driving accident. The defendant stated that he has one handicap that he is aware of, he is a slow learner."

Smith told his probation officer, Joann King, that he began abusing alcohol at age fourteen. He had also used marijuana. By age seventeen he was drinking on a daily basis but stopped drinking in 1990. King wrote, "The defendant stated that he used marijuana approximately one time a week. He stated that when he was approximately thirty years of age, he stopped using that controlled substance. The defendant stated he has suffered blackouts and memory loss commonly associated with the long-term abuse of drugs and alcohol." King's opinion was that Smith "may have minimized his use, due to [wanting to] look favorably to this officer."

She added another observation. "Although the defendant has a learning handicap, the defendant has the ability to remember dates very well, without difficulty at all."

Having interviewed and investigated Smith, Joann King submitted her report to the Court, which stated in part, "It is the opinion of the Probation Department there is a substantial risk the defendant will commit further crimes contrary to Indiana statute." She reported that, with all factors considered, "The defendant is in need of correctional treatment that can best be provided by his commitment to a penal facility." She asked the Court to accept the plea agreement offered by the Prosecutor's office.

The plea bargain called for Smith to spend thirty-eight years locked up in prison. Smith later declared that his attorney urged him to accept the deal. "He come over there, Dave Whitton told me," Smith related, "he goes, uh go, he says plead guilty to it. He said they got Ralph Jacobs going in to appear in Court against you and he gone to finger you."

On December 13, 1991, ten months after the murder, Christopher Smith signed a plea agreement that he could neither read nor understand. The agreement said that he waived the State and Federal rights guaranteed him.

The rights he waived stated, "The Defendant understands that the State and Federal Constitutions guarantee all criminal defendants certain rights, among them being a public trial by jury, to a speedy trial, to be free from self-incrimination, to confront and cross-examine the State's witnesses, to have compulsory process for obtaining witnesses for the Defense, and to require the State to prove guilt beyond a reasonable doubt."

With all his rights voided by his signature, Smith also acknowledged that his guilty plea was all the proof needed to make him a convicted killer. The document read in part, "The defendant further understands that the entry of a guilty plea pursuant to this agreement waives those rights and... that guilty plea amounts to a conviction."

The words sounded harsh when read aloud in court. Smith, of course, could read nothing from the pages he signed. He only knew that his attorney, David Whitton, told him to take the plea rather than risk a sentence of sixty years.

Reasons he later gave for signing the agreement were that he understood that he would definitely get sixty years if he went before a jury and he thought prison would be a better place than the county jail. Smith wanted to be moved from the Henry County Jail. "They treated us like dogs and cats over there," he struggled to explain, "No hot water. Half the toilets didn't work."

He also believed that by going away to prison he was protecting his sister, Wyona, and her two children.

After he'd signed the plea bargain, probation officer Joann King visited Smith in jail. "I told her I didn't do it. She said you can't plead guilty to something you didn't do," Smith related. "And I just, and she was getting kind of upset and I was too. And I was tired. I said yes I done it." He shrugged, and paused. "And she just got up and left."

Sentencing was set for January 16, 1992, at 9:00 a.m. The Probation Department believed there was a substantial risk that Smith would commit further crimes if he were not incarcerated. He was a follower who could be led to participate in worse crimes. They stated that his crime was "aggravating in nature, in that, no individual has the right to take away the life of another human being." The sentencing hearing was just a formality. Smith had already signed thirty-eight years of his life away.

Smith was taken to the Pendleton Reformatory. Mentally, he was trampled by a nervous breakdown and he suffered from lack of sleep. Haunted by the realization that he might never again see his son, his siblings, or his young niece and nephew, Christopher Smith went into lockdown, still not understanding why he was being punished for a murder he did not commit.

CHAPTER 10—PERCY'S FEARSOME HOUSE GUEST

Douglas Percy met Jerry Thompson in September of 1990 through a mutual acquaintance, Mark Phillips. Phillips asked Percy if Thompson could use his garage and tools to replace a muffler. Percy agreed. "I had the jacks and everything to do that," he recalled.

Thompson brought the car to Percy's house but the next day had to go get a muffler. "First he took off the old one. Then he went to the junkyard and bought a muffler." Percy recalled. "He came back and went to put it on and he needed a sleeve. I did not have a sleeve. He did not have money to buy a sleeve."

After the car sat on Percy's property for a couple of weeks, he said, "He came back one day and he picked up the car and said he was going to drive it back off to where he bought it from because he could not make the payments on it." They put the muffler on, "but we could not drive it because it would fall off," Percy explained.

The friendship built through the repair of a number of destitute vehicles. In November, Thompson arrived with his girlfriend, Shawn McCormick, in a '74 white Ford pickup. She had been driving a second pickup, a burgundy and white one, and it expired on the freeway near Percy's house. They asked for Percy's help.

Percy tried every form of mechanical first aid he knew, but he could not start the truck. Plus, one tire and the spare were both flat.

The burgundy and white pickup took up residence in Percy's backyard and the two men worked on it for weeks, drinking beer together and talking. On weekends, Thompson brought Shawn over to play cards with Percy and his wife, Jerra. The couples got along well.

In mid to late January of 1991, Shawn and Jerry needed a place to stay. Doug and Jerra Percy invited them in. "They could not live at his brother's house," Percy explained, "because Shawn and his brother's girlfriend, Dee, did not get along. She was going to move to her mother's house and he was going to move to his brother's house. She was crying."

The arrangement was nothing new. The Percys had often allowed another of Doug's friends, Mike Featheringill, to stay with them "every time he would get in a fight with his girlfriend," Percy said. Doug and Jerra Percy had four daughters, aged thirteen and ten, and eight-year-old twins; but they always found room in their home for friends.

Shawn maintained her job at the Shell station, working nights and sleeping days. Jerry Thompson worked sporadically for his brother Steve, who owned a machine shop.

Percy and Thompson began working on trucks together. Percy said, "We made a good team. What I could not pick up, he could. What I could not break loose, he could. Where he could not reach, I could. It worked for us good." Normally they each worked on their own vehicles with help from the other, but they also sometimes did work for others for pay.

After Crandall's robbery and murder, Thompson cut up the shotgun, the M-10, "and I think the revolver," Percy said. Thompson kept the remaining guns, including the Stallard 9mm semi-automatic, in his bedroom dresser. He sold the pot. They weighed it on an electronic scale in

Percy's bedroom. He had salvaged the scale from the trash at work and repaired it. Percy estimated that the take was a pound of marijuana and that Thompson sold half a pound to his brother.

It was the end of the workday at Hillis Auto Sales when Thompson and Percy arrived on March 14, 1991. The place was near Percy's job and he wanted to look at a black Riviera. Thompson remained outside while Percy went into the sales office. The two salesmen inside were snug at their desks, avoiding the door and the March weather outside it. They offered Percy the key to the car and invited him to inspect it.

Percy looked over the car and liked it, but felt that the price was a little high. He discovered a flaw, a leaking gasket, and tried to barter down the price. The two salesmen laughed him off, saying they could easily fix such a small problem.

Percy returned their key but went out to look over the car again and consider it some more. Then he saw Thompson going into the office and decided to follow. Maybe his buddy could work a deal for him.

Thompson stepped through the door with Percy behind him and fired the 9mm handgun at the first man behind his desk. It took several shots to kill him. The second man dove to the floor, but Thompson leaned down and shot him in the face.

While the men's hearts fluttered with final beats, Thompson grappled with their bodies, seizing wallets and keys from their pockets. He threw these items into the center of the floor and ordered Percy to pick them up. "Open up that file cabinet, see if there's money in there." Percy obeyed quickly. The drawers did not stick as Crandall's refrigerator had, but he found no other cash. The two drove away in Thompson's El Dorado.

"No witnesses, no problems." Thompson's mantra was supposed to be reassuring to the smaller man, but Percy felt the shadow of his own death coming. There was one witness.

Him. And he cowered, wondering when his neck would be broken, when his body would be ripped apart with bullets.

***

Thompson continued to live with the Percy family, but after the murders, the camaraderie between the two men was gone. Percy watched Thompson's every move with dread, fearing that not even his little ones were safe from the savagery of the beast he had brought into his home.

Despite his fear, Percy also viewed Thompson as a powerful ally. Three months after the Crandall murder, Percy found himself stiffed for $5,000. He had signed a bond to bail a friend, David Van Horn, out of jail. Van Horn left jail and fled the state. Percy had heard that he went to Houston, Texas, and he intended to go after him. If he took Thompson along, he surely would come back with either the fugitive or his money.

Thompson debated whether or not to go along but Percy, aware of his inability to make the long drive alone, convinced him to go. Percy covered the expenses. Thompson insisted on taking a gun. "Jerry said he did not want to go without it," Percy explained. "He said if he backs him up in a corner, he wants to have something to protect himself with."

Just a few miles from home, as they were moving onto the freeway, Percy learned that a second gun was also in the van but he did not turn around. "Jerry was not going to take it back," he said. Although they had no permits to carry guns, Percy kept driving.

They traveled safely to Houston but their search for the fugitive was fruitless. Percy said, "I talked to his brother-in-law. He was there, every place I was he was there the day before." Their failure to find Van Horn cost Percy $5,000 for the bond and an additional $2,000 in attorney's fees.

On the way home, the two were stopped by a trooper in Illinois. The guns! "You got to take the blame," Thompson told Percy. He was not going back to prison.

Percy tried to deny that there were guns in the van but ended up signing the consent form. "They said if they did not search the vehicle, they were going to impound it and search anyway," he explained later.

Percy was arrested by Illinois State Police for possession of the two guns. There was an M-11, a machine gun type weapon beneath the passenger's seat and a 9mm pistol in a storage compartment below the dashboard on the passenger's side. He was also cited for speeding, driving without a seatbelt, and being in possession of an unregistered vehicle.

He and Thompson owned the vehicle together. They had bought it through a *Trader* magazine from an out-of-business cleaning company. They paid $300 cash for it but that company had never registered it.

Later, at the police station, Percy heard a message over the police broadcast unit that they were searching for a light-colored van believed to be carrying a pool table stolen from a downtown pool hall. He claimed that he had not been speeding at all but paid the fine because, "I fought a couple speeding tickets and you do not win anyway."

Percy knew how the system worked. He had previous arrests in Indiana for altering vehicle identification numbers and public intoxication.

The two returned to Percy's home. Despite his faithfulness in "taking the blame" for the guns, Percy was still walking on shattered glass around Thompson. His wife and daughters, who knew nothing about the Crandall murder, quickly realized that, no matter what Thompson said or did, their dad was not going to defend them or even speak up for them.

The tension did not ease until midsummer when Thompson and Shawn broke up. She moved out and Thompson moved in with another woman. He still kept Percy on a short leash, though, and frequently dropped in on his partner in crime.

Percy was careful to make the big man welcome, even though he had many reasons to be nervous.

CHAPTER 11—BODY COUNT RISING

On September 4, 1991, twenty-nine-year-old Kathy Boggs and thirty-nine-year-old Allen White went into the Hustler Bar to see Jerry Thompson. Witnesses stated that Kathy was there to talk to Thompson about some money he owed her.

The couple was later found in a car parked in a garage behind a residence at 1325 North LaSalle Street, both dead from gunshot wounds to the head. Jerry Thompson's fingerprints were found on the outside of the vehicle.

No charges were filed. There was not enough evidence to get a conviction—but there was talk.

One police report stated that, "Mrs. Betty Booher told investigators that on September 12, '91, she overheard a conversation between Thompson and Shawn McCormick, in which Thompson stated, 'he had done the couple in the bar and left their bodies in the car dead.'"

Doug Percy heard about the murders too. His information came straight from Thompson, who came to Percy's house a few days after the killings and announced to his old friend that he had shot the two victims. He seemed to relish Percy's jumpy responses as he shared details of the killings.

***

Then, Jerry Thompson and Douglas Percy were both arrested for altering vehicle identification numbers. Percy was released on bail, but Thompson was held because he was still on parole. Locked inside a jail cell, he could not lay hands on Percy nor his family. But he called and kept calling, threatening what he would do if Percy did not keep silent.

Douglas Michael Percy had never been a hero. Born April 15, 1954, in Buffalo, New York, he grew up in Florida and California, graduating from high school in San Fernando in 1972. He began working in plating during high school. At one time, Percy tried to enlist in the United States Navy but was turned down. His physical revealed a macular scar on one eye. "They said it looked like a sunburn."

During a ten-year period, he was arrested for driving under the influence of alcohol and borderline reckless driving. He left California in 1981, moving to Indiana near his wife's parents' home.

In his police photos, Percy does not look like an actor one would choose to play the role of a criminal. A short-necked man with thick wavy hair and a cropped beard lining his jawbone, he looks more like a bystander. But Thompson's threats against his family boiled his blood into an ounce of courage.

CHAPTER 12—STATE'S WITNESS: DOUGLAS PERCY

On March 18, 1992, Percy walked into Indianapolis police headquarters to tell them everything he knew about Jerry Thompson.

His story was interesting but became credible when Percy gave the Indianapolis Police Department their best evidence yet. He sketched the New Castle crime scene showing the layout of Crandall's kitchen and the position of the body. The drawing left no doubt that he'd been there. He indicated himself along one wall of the kitchen in front of the refrigerator and Crandall on the opposite side, lying dead beside the stove.

Most chilling was that his depiction of the victim looked like a preschooler's scribble but he took care in drawing a knife with the word "Tiger" adorning the handle. This knife, known by investigators to be missing from the murder scene, was given to Percy by Thompson.

Percy's March 18, 1992, eyewitness statement sent officers scurrying for evidence. Percy told officers about the guns that had been taken from him in Illinois. He believed his record was expunged from the weapons possession charge because he had no repeated arrests within a six-month period, but Illinois had made no mention of returning the guns to him.

On March 19, Indianapolis Police Department Sergeant David E. Phillips and Detective Thomas Minor retrieved from the Illinois State Police the murder weapon, a black Stallard 9mm semi-automatic pistol. They also took custody of the other weapon taken from Percy at the time of his arrest, a gray SWD 9mm Mac-11 semi-automatic pistol.

Both guns were turned over to Evan Thompson, a forensic scientist, employed by the crime lab. He performed multiple ballistics tests and confirmed that the Stallard was the murder weapon used to kill the men at Hillis Auto.

CHAPTER 13—NO JUSTICE FOR THE OPPRESSED

New Castle law enforcement responded to Percy's statement with a new investigation into Junior Crandall's murder. They went to the Branchville Training Center where Ralph Jacobs Jr. was imprisoned. They had questions.

With the impetus of Percy's confession, Ralph Jacobs Jr. found that law enforcement was finally listening to him. Jacobs now claimed that Stephens threatened to have his ailing father arrested for lying to the police. He said that Stephens threw things (though not at him) and called him a liar.

Jacobs also asserted that Stephens made harassing telephone calls to his family members. He said, "The more I cooperated the less my family got harassed." Even later, during court appearances, Jacobs had not spoken up about his ordeal with Stephens in the room for fear the harassment would start again.

Now that he was no longer under Stephens's power, Jacobs related that during interrogation Stephens "started telling me how" the events of the murder transpired and "then they'd turn on the tape player and have me tell it."

The public was finally made aware that Jacobs was a mentally handicapped man who could neither read nor write. When law enforcement first picked him up for questioning, he had tried to deny the charge, saying he'd never been to

Crandall's home and that he was at his parents' house at the time of the murder.

But the questioning continued for hours each day, newspapers informed a shocked community. Jacobs was told that he was lying. That there were witnesses. That he was intimidated and told that his terminally ill father would be arrested for lying to the cops. He had no way to determine if the threat could be carried out and he was told he did not need a lawyer.

Though he knew nothing about the murder, Jacobs had confessed, agreeing that he held Crandall down and placed a pillow over his head while the triggerman shot him.

Smith and Jacobs were strangers to each other; they had a nodding acquaintance from being on occasion in the same tavern. Neither of them claimed to know the decedent nor any details of the murder.

Smith had a similar tale of woe. He had insisted from the beginning that he was at his sister's house when the murder occurred. Smith said he refused to confess until Detective Jim Stephens threatened his sister, saying he would have her arrested and her children turned over to the Welfare Department.

"Jim Stephens told us the details, told us what to say," Smith reported.

Faced with accusations, intimidation, witnesses, and tapes, both Jacobs and Smith had uttered coerced confessions, saying that they were the men who murdered Wesley Crandall. A barbaric twist of the legal system had "proved" both men were guilty of murder.

***

On April 23, 1992, Detective Richard Shoemaker of the Indiana State Police and Captain Butch Baker of the New Castle Police Department reopened the investigation of Crandall's murder. Indianapolis Homicide Detectives gave them a history of the case along with photographs of Thompson and Percy.

On May 29, 1992, Baker and Shoemaker interviewed Ralph's mother, Janet Jacobs. She insisted that Ralph was home the night of Crandall's murder.

The officers asked specifically about guns in the house. "Were the guns there that night? Taken out of the gun cabinet for any reason?" the officers asked.

"No. They were not," Janet asserted. "One is an antique. It's never out of there and the other one is Ralph Sr.'s hunting gun and it stays there also until Ralph Sr. takes it out." Janet told them that her husband, who had died six months earlier, had not hunted for some time, but from the time they married, he'd blasted a shotgun up into the air on New Year's Eve. Since Ralph Sr. died, the guns had been locked in a gun cabinet with the key in a drawer out of the reach of the grandchildren.

Shoemaker asked, "Would there be any problem if you let Captain Baker look at those shotguns? And got our word to give them back to you? Because I imagine they're keepsakes."

"They're not going to leave the house," Janet replied. "You can look at 'em but he's not taking them out of the house."

The investigators asked the mother, why had Ralph told police he was involved in the Crandall murder?

"Because that was the deal to get him four years instead of forty," Janet told them, "since they was gonna lock him up anyway. That's what the lawyer told him to say." When she talked to Ralph's attorney, Randy Sorrell, about the plea, Janet said, "I didn't want to go for it, I wanted to go to trial. But they went on this other plea-bargaining deal on both Chris Smith and Ralph. And I really don't think either one of 'em is guilty. I know Ralph's not. I just feel Chris has gotten hog washed into this too, because he's retarded and he's slow and it's a couple of dumb guys that got hooked into it."

Baker asked, "At any time did you ever come into an office like this and talk to police officers? Did they ever take a statement from you? How about Ralph Sr.?"

"Nope." Ralph Sr. had come up one time and "All he said was that Stephens called him a 'fucking liar.' Ralph Sr. and Ralph Jr. Those were his exact words." Janet said she didn't use "potty words" herself, but that was what the man said. Bursting to finally tell her side of the story, Janet ranted, "And Ralph Jr. kept telling me that Stephens kept, had a tape recorder going and he kept turning it on and then turning it off."

When he turned it off, Ralph had told his mother, Stephens would threaten him. He would never tell her what those threats were. After he was arrested, she was not allowed to see her son for a month.

No one would listen to the truth, she said. "Police. Stephens or any of 'em. They say he's guilty and that's it. Got down to where he'll serve four years, and he's trying his best to stay on good behavior to get out when he's supposed to. I need him at home."

***

On June 25, 1992, Ralph's uncle, Levi Jacobs, was interviewed at the Navistar Factory on Brookville Road by Captain Baker and Detective Shoemaker. Levi had not seen his nephew since the night he was arrested. Levi said his brother, Ralph's father, "didn't talk about it much but I mean it hurt him…because I mean we know he didn't do it and it hit him so hard I mean I think that's got a little bit to do with where he's at now." Levi said his brother died on December 5, 1991, eight days before his birthday.

"And here's another thing. I want to add this," Levi said. "You know you remember the jacket that they said he was wearing; you know that brown jacket? All right. They still got it. Well that jacket belongs to me. That jacket was hanging in my closet and been hanging there for at least two weeks."

When the police demanded the jacket, it was handed over "because I figured that they would come up there and say no this is not the jacket and I would get it back." But police simply took the jacket and asked Levi no questions. If they had, he would have asserted that he had never seen Ralph's hand on a gun.

* * *

Baker and Shoemaker's findings, in regard to Ralph Jacobs Jr. were that, "despite his guilty plea in this cause, he did not, in fact, commit the offense of Battery as indicated at the Guilty Plea Hearing and thus he had, in fact, no personal knowledge of the circumstances surrounding the death of Wesley Crandall Jr.

"He indicated that he had signed the Plea Agreement and admitted to having committed such offense due to the fact that law enforcement authorities had threatened him and his family and, further, due to his fear that, if he went to trial, he would be convicted of the greater charge of Aiding in the Commission of the Offense of Murder."

CHAPTER 14—A MULTIMILLION-DOLLAR MISTAKE

On July 27, 1992, the State responded to Ralph Jacob's file for Post-Conviction Relief. Malcolm K. Edwards, Prosecuting Attorney for the 53rd Judicial Circuit Court of Indiana said that in regard to the shooting death of Wesley Crandall, "subsequent investigation revealed the existence of evidence of material facts not previously presented and heard." He cited Douglas Percy's statements on May 12 and 13, 1992, saying that "Percy was present when one Jerry K. Thompson shot and killed Wesley Crandall Jr."

He further noted, "That investigators have confirmed numerous representations made by Percy, and the State has now filed formal charges against Jerry K. Thompson for said matter. That the State is satisfied that Ralph Jacobs Jr. did not kill Crandall and was not present when Crandall was shot." The Court was asked to grant Post-Conviction Relief to Jacobs.

Ralph sweltered in prison for another week, awaiting his day in court. On August 4, 1992, he appeared in the Henry County Superior Court, again accompanied by his public defender, Randall V. Sorrell.

Court records summarized Jacobs's plea agreement of October 15, 1991, which declared that Jacobs had been required to give a truthful account of Crandall's murder and would receive "imposition of a fully aggravated sentence" of eight years.

In considering Jacobs's plea for Post-Conviction Relief, it was noted that, "The Court finds that both the defendant-petitioner and his alleged accomplice, Christopher C. Smith, are of less-than-normal mental functioning ability and are, as a result, prone to misrepresentations, misstatements, and misunderstandings of facts and circumstances. Clearly all evidence now leaves to only find and conclude that, based on the newly discovered evidence…the defendant-petitioner… was not truthful to the Court."

The Court granted Jacobs's petition but further declared that, "Notwithstanding such actions, the defendant-petitioner, Ralph A. Jacobs Jr., shall remain incarcerated in the Henry County Jail until such time as the State, as indicated by the Prosecuting Attorney, tenders to the Court its Motion to Dismiss and the Court, in turn, rules on that motion as currently envisioned by all concerned."

Jacobs returned to jail to await the paperwork. Not understanding the process, he worried that the judge would keep him locked up because he'd been forced to lie. He was back in Henry County but still a long way from home.

Both Jacobs and Smith had spent a year in the Henry County Jail before they were turned over to the Department of Corrections. According to an *Indianapolis Star* article published November 8, 1992, "During that time, Jacobs… learned of his fifty-six-year-old father's death from sleep apnea. Jailers allowed him to attend the funeral for about ten minutes—in shackles."

Attorney David Neal filed a lawsuit on behalf of Chris Smith. He said of Smith and Jacobs, "These are gentle people." He was horrified that the two men had been held, defenseless captives of the justice system, for eighteen months.

Christopher Smith's release was abrupt. He arrived at the Henry County Police Department still wearing his prison uniform with his prisoner number on it. There, he was informed that his personal belongings, including his clothing, had been lost. Neal said, "His wallet, which contained no money but did contain some identification at the time of his arrest, had been lost. So, Monday at 9:30 a.m. Chris was given a trash bag to put his current Department of Corrections clothing in and was sent home wearing a county DOC shirt and DOC jeans, with the numbers still on them.

"He didn't have a penny in his pocket and didn't have any identification," Neal related. Even though he had a disability that hindered his walking, Smith was told by authorities to walk home. With no funds to even make a phone call, the newly freed prisoner was forced to hobble across town to his sister's house on his painfully swollen leg. "He was not given clothing, the dignity or even the offer of a ride after what he'd been through," Neal continued.

As Smith made his way home along Broad Street toward his sister's home, Neal said, "according to my client, a police officer involved in the investigation last year pulled up to him and told him he'd better not see him out after dark."

Smith's new life as a free man didn't offer much promise.

Neal said of Smith, "After what has been done to my client by certain officials, the last thing he should have to put up with is their rude and callous remarks." If the aggravation continued, Neal said he would seek, "protective orders, civil rights injunctions, and assistance of federal authorities if that's what it takes to protect my client."

An *Indianapolis Star* article stated that "Neal has notified the City, Henry County, and the State of a pending $50.9 million-dollar lawsuit on behalf of Smith for civil rights violations, false arrest, and false imprisonment." An identical lawsuit would be filed on Ralph Jacobs's behalf by Muncie Attorney Michael J. Alexander.

Jim Stephens's response was nonplussed. He said, "We investigated the case the same as any other case is investigated."

Jacobs's mother expired from heart problems one month after his release from prison. He moved in with his sister and resumed his passion for TV and collecting baseball cards.

Smith also moved in with his sister, Wyona. Both Chris and Wyona suffered from neurofibromatosis dubbed "Elephant Man's Disease." A growth on Chris's left leg caused a permanent limp. The moment he was released, Chris had one mission in mind. He wanted to buy Christmas presents for his niece and nephew.

When the lawsuit was settled, Smith was awarded $605,000. Jacobs received $435,000. Neither man lived long enough to enjoy this monetary justice. Health issues and the traumas of prison took them both to early graves.

CHAPTER 15—FOUR GRAVES IN INDIANAPOLIS

With Smith and Jacobs cleared of Crandall's murder, energies turned to proving that Jerry Thompson had committed the crime. Investigators also needed to prove that Jacobs and Smith had solid alibis and could not be set forth to elicit reasonable doubt in the jury.

Shoemaker and Baker interviewed Doug Percy at the Indianapolis Police Department on May 12, 1992, at 10:00 a.m. Attorney Thomas Thomas was present. On tape, Percy described the events that were a prelude to Crandall's gruesome death. He described Crandall's murder and related that one of the guns stolen from that murder was used in the Hillis Auto murders. Percy said that he had no reason to lie about the New Castle homicide.

Percy's account was that two weeks before the Crandall murder, Jerry Thompson, his brother Dave Thompson, and Percy drove from Indianapolis to New Castle to meet with a person called "Dave." Percy described Dave as a stocky white male who owned a Chevy Camaro. Dave was in the kitchen of his residence working on the motor, a 350 engine.

Dave drove with the three men to a drug dealer's house. "Stay in the truck," Dave told Percy. "Too many people coming at the door at once will spook this guy." Percy complied. The other three men entered the residence and when they returned, Dave told Percy, "Jerry did himself some big business today, sold some marijuana to that dealer slick as a whistle."

That wasn't the only drug deal of the day, Percy recalled. Thompson entered into another transaction with "Bobby," another New Castle resident. Bobby gave Thompson $600 in cash, in return for which, Thompson was to supply him with some cocaine. Thompson crushed some pills, creating a fake bag of cocaine.

On February 12, 1991, Percy rode with Thompson and his girlfriend, Shawn McCormick, to deliver the false drug. "He'll never know," Thompson assured them. "Bobby's brain dead."

Bobby's house, near a railroad track, was in a rundown area of businesses and residences. Percy was short on details but recalled that the man lived on a busy street with an automatic signal nearby.

Bobby was not home. Thompson drove over to check another location and then decided to disregard the delivery. He had Bobby's $600. The trio went to Kmart where Shawn used part of the $600 to purchase a shotgun while Thompson bought two wristwatches. They returned to Indianapolis.

Later that day, Bobby and a male passenger arrived at Percy's house in a Chevette. Bobby approached the house, gun in hand, determined that he would not leave without either his money or his drugs. Thompson accepted the challenge from Percy's doorway. He blasted his new shotgun at the car. Bobby leaped back into the car and the two men sped away. Percy said he never saw them again.

Two days later, on the day of the murder, Thompson and Percy again drove to New Castle to see about a drug deal with the man "Dave" had introduced Thompson to. They drove to Crandall's house but he was not at home. They meandered around town for a while, stopping at a Village Pantry convenience store. They also went to visit Thompson's brother in Mount Summit. The brother was not home.

This left them with nothing to do. They found a wooded area uphill from the State Road 3 in an area signed "Spiceland." In these isolated woods they test-fired the shotgun several times.

The gun worked fine. A few hours later, it would blast Wesley Crandall into eternity.

Thompson cut through a park and slid off the road. The truck stuck and after jolting the truck back and forth a dozen times, they worked it loose and got back on the main road. The two men stopped for beer and cigarettes. Then it was time to go looking for Crandall again.

Crandall was home, and happy to see them. He would be dead within minutes.

After the murder Percy kept quiet for ten months. Then around the first of the year in 1992, he was in his garage, drinking, and talking to his buddy, Mike Featheringill. He confided in Featheringill about the New Castle homicide. "I don't know what to do, Mike. I don't think I can do anything. Down to my bones, I am terrified of Jerry Thompson." Featheringill related this conversation in a taped interview with law enforcement on May 12, 1992. His story matched Percy's.

The next day, May 13, Shoemaker and Baker met Percy at the junctures of State Road 3 and I-70. They wanted Percy to try to lead them to the places he had mentioned in his taped statement. "I think I can find Spiceland," Percy offered. He indicated the area where they had fired the shotgun, County Road 200 South, west of State Road 3 and east of Spiceland Pike. They found the yellow Spiceland Road sign Percy had noted at the intersection of State Road 3 and Trojan Lane.

Percy viewed New Castle Police Department mug books and identified "Bobby" as Bobby West, DOB January 3, 1961. "He was the person who gave Thompson $600 cash for the cocaine and who was later shot at by Thompson on the road in front of my house," Percy said.

He also identified the Camaro owner, Murrell David Loveless II, DOB August 27, 1963, as the person who introduced the Thompson brothers to Wesley Crandall.

Officers Shoemaker and Baker, armed with Bobby West's address, 1338 South 18th Street, meandered through several areas in New Castle. They asked Percy to identify any residences that matched the places he'd been. Percy appeared lost and then pointed suddenly. "That one." Percy had correctly identified Bobby's residence in the area near 14th Street and "I" Avenue.

He did not locate "Dave's" home. He said that he had only been there once and it was dark.

Percy gave another taped statement on May 13, 1992. The second statement was given in the presence of his lawyer again and was a remake of the May 12 tape, which had malfunctioned.

Baker and Shoemaker found "Dave," David Loveless. They determined that he lived at 713 North 25th Street and had owned a red Camaro in January, 1991. On May 15, 1992, Baker interviewed Loveless. Video and audio tapes were made of that interview.

Loveless stated that weeks before the murder, David and Jerry Thompson contacted him and asked for his help with a drug deal. He agreed and took the brothers to Crandall's residence where he introduced the men to each other.

A drug transaction ensued but Loveless did not know the particulars of who bought what. He did not remember Doug Percy nor any other individual being there.

Crandall and Loveless had been friends for a long time. Loveless was able to describe some of Crandall's guns, including a chrome .38 or 357 revolver with the words "Pit Bull" or possibly "Bull Dog" on it.

Later that day, Bobby G. West met investigators Shoemaker and Baker at the New Castle Police Department. In his deposition, West stated that he had given Thompson $600 for cocaine and that Thompson never delivered. West and his buddy, David Prince, drove to a house off Post Road where Thompson was staying with a person named Doug. Prince stayed inside West's 1979 gray Chevy Chevette while West approached the house.

West said that Jerry Thompson appeared at the front door, racking a shotgun. Thompson pointed the shotgun at West and West pointed a handgun at Thompson. West retreated but Thompson discharged the shotgun at the driver's door of the Chevette. Prince picked Bobby up and they left the area.

Investigators were directed to West's sister's residence. The inoperable Chevette was parked in her backyard. They photographed damage to the driver's door just below the side mirror "that would be consistent with being shot with a shotgun."

One more piece of evidence for the file, but it would take a shovelful of puzzle pieces to back up Percy's remarkable story.

Mark Winchester's statement on May 18, 1992 was that, "I was at Junior's home just before the murder. He sold me $60 worth of marijuana. Two other guys showed up and I left. I passed this one guy and he looked like 'Smitty' Chris Smith. It looked like him, you know. But I didn't see the guy walk. Can't say if he walked with a limp." Winchester was not able to identify the person he saw from photo arrays.

Gladys Case was also reinterviewed on May 19, 1992. She repeated her story from the evening of the murder. She had never met Wolfman "But I've seen him around, ever since I was fourteen." She indicated that the photo of Douglas Percy "looked like Wolfman but Wolfman's hair is fuller." Shown the original photo array from 1991, Mrs. Case again identified Ralph "Wolfman" Jacobs Jr. as the man she saw that night.

Investigators called in Crandall's friends and former apartment dwellers: David Fitzpatrick, Regina Fitzpatrick, Jack Ford, Anna Stewart, Jeffrey Howe, Ralph Eugene Davis, Sandra K. Walker, Frank Barber, and Hollis Pierce.

All knew Crandall well and had frequented his residence. Several were able to describe Crandall's weapons. A few knew who Smith or Jacobs were. Smith had spent time with Jack Ford but had never been known to sell drugs for anyone. None of Crandall's acquaintances had ever known of Chris Smith or Ralph Jacobs Jr. to be at Crandall's home.

Only Barber said that he "had seen Ralph Jacobs at, or around Crandall's residence several times prior to Crandall being killed." Hollis Pierce said he'd seen Jacobs at a local tavern, the Twilight, trying to sell photos.

With this investigation behind them, Baker and Shoemaker went to take another statement from Ralph Jacobs.

But when Baker and Shoemaker approached him on May 26, 1992, Ralph Jacobs refused to speak with them. He insisted that his attorney, Randy Sorrell, be called first. With Sorrell's permission, the two investigators obtained a fresh statement from Jacobs and made audio and video tapes of it.

The former prisoner told them the same story he had tried to communicate the previous year: "I did not know Crandall. I never been to Crandall's house. And I did not kill the man!" He never saw Charlie Alcorn before February 14, 1991, and then only because Jim Stephens pointed him out. He also advised the officers that Stephens had "threatened him into saying what he wanted him to say."

Baker and Shoemaker next spoke with Chris Smith. Step by step, Smith told the investigators the events of his days surrounding the murders. He had walked around town all day: to his sister's house, the Twilight, and his brother's house. "I went back to my place around 1:00 [p.m.]."

Smith counted off the remainder of the day on his fingers. "I picked up sodas and carried them to my sister's house. Then I walked Rebecca home from school and I ate dinner with Tracy and Wyona and Rebecca and William." This was about 5:30 p.m.

"After that I helped Mr. Razor fill a pop machine and went home. Sometime later I went back to the Twilight

Bar. People there were saying that police were looking for Wolfman." Smith stayed at the bar until closing, and then walked home.

The day after the murder, "Mr. Razor, he took me over to Muncie for divorce court. You can check. I was there. We got back about 3:00 o'clock." Then Smith cleaned up and went to his sister's house. He stayed for supper. He spent his evening at the Twilight. "I sold my shotgun, a 20 gauge to Lillian Foster for twenty-five dollars. I bought the shotgun from Lillian a month before, but she wanted it back and I needed the money."

On February 16th, Smith went to Monticello, Kentucky, with Mr. Gregory. "Next day I come back to New Castle and went to visit my friend, Jack Ford. He told me that the police were looking for me. I called the police from Ford's house." Then he waited.

Police officers picked Smith up from Ford's house without incident. He was interviewed at police headquarters by Stephens and Sergeant Cronk of the Henry County Drug Task Force. Smith maintained that he did not commit the crime.

"I never known Crandall," Smith told Baker and Shoemaker, "but I confessed because I was threatened by Stephens." He said Stephens would tell him what to say, and then turn the tape on and record it.

The investigative report read: "Smith stated that he was told by Stephens that he [Smith] had killed Crandall for some money that Crandall owed him. He was then told to tell about the drug deal. Even though there was no drug deal, Smith in an attempt to protect his sister, Wyona, and her children from Detective Stephens, repeated the story. When asked by Detective Stephens who dropped the marijuana off which Crandall was to pay [Smith] for, he told the Detectives that Tom Haskett delivered the marijuana."

During the May 26, 1992, interview, Smith was asked where the name Tom Haskett came from. Smith said he made it up. It was later learned that Tom Haskett was the name of the man who ran off with Smith's ex-wife, Nancy Smith, and stole his pickup truck. Haskett was in jail for failure to pay child support.

Following these interviews, a team of officers including Shoemaker and Baker converged on Doug Percy's residence on May 28, 1992, search warrant in hand. They wanted clear evidence of Percy's story, better yet, the shotgun or pieces of the shotgun used to murder Crandall. The search focused in and around Percy's garage.

Percy gave the searchers a silencer and a strap that Thompson had left behind. "He tried to burn up stuff in here," Percy told them, and directed them to a fuel oil tank in the yard that had been converted to a stove for burning. Sifting through debris and ashes, they found: an ammo box lid, charred wood, a threaded bolt, a Charter Arms, and a Pachmayr handgun grip.

Investigators dug up Percy's driveway and pried into his garage walls. They found scattered chunks of destroyed weapons just as Percy had described. The evidence appeared ample to support Percy's story. The shotgun that killed Crandall had been destroyed but recognizable pieces were found. There was no link between the pieces they found and the two suspects, Smith and Jacobs, and no reason to believe that the falsely accused men had ever handled the murder weapon.

With this evidence in hand, Baker and Shoemaker went back to New Castle to ask the questions that would support their new theory in a court of law.

CHAPTER 16—NEW TALES FROM OLD TESTIMONIES

On May 29, 1992, Smith's sister, Wyona Alton, confirmed Smith's story that he had been at her home watching *Full House* when the murder was committed. "I told those detectives he had been there, watching that show, and that they called me a liar," she complained.

Glenda Lee, a former employee of the Speedway convenience store at 18th and Broadway, had told police that on the evening of the murder, Wolfman had entered the store, bought a pack of Winston cigarettes, and left on foot. She also reconfirmed her story on May 29.

Later that day, the officers spoke with Ralph Jacobs's mother, Janet Jacobs. She told them that except for walking to a local store, Ralph was home the night of Crandall's murder. They got a statement from Dr. Grant's office, verifying that Ralph's sister, Loretta Cooper, had been seen by the doctor the day of the murder. They also obtained weather reports for February 14, 1991, from the National Weather Service.

On June 2, 1992, Sergeant Mark James of the Indiana State Police administered polygraph tests to Doug Percy, Chris Smith, and Ralph Jacobs Jr. Smith passed his polygraph and the examiner, Mark J. James, Laboratory Division, Indiana State Police sent his analysis saying, "Physiological responses noted on this subject's polygraph charts are in such a pattern as to cause this examiner to believe that Mr.

Smith did not shoot Wesley Crandall and should be cleared from this investigation."

Smith's previous polygraph, administered by Ed Davis, also of the Indiana State Police, had a different result on March 15, 1991. In that test, Smith's "No" response to question three, "Do you know for sure who shot Junior?" elicited "specific reactions," according to the examiner and because of this supposed knowledge, he said, Smith "cannot be cleared as having told the complete truth during his examination."

Jacobs's results were inconclusive.

Doug Percy, who was examined by James the same day, was also not cleared. Based on the charts, "It is the opinion of this examiner that the subject has not been completely truthful," he stated. "Mr. Percy has not told the entire truth concerning shooting Wesley Crandall and cannot be cleared from this investigation."

The next day, June 3, officers spoke with Nancy Smith, Chris's ex-wife. Young Christopher Smith, aged twenty-two months, was with her during the interview. The couple married in January of 1990, and divorced on February 15, 1991.

Nancy Smith had never known Chris to use or sell marijuana. "He didn't have any drug money," Nancy told the detectives. "Smitty received Social Security benefits and made some side money by doing odd jobs and yard maintenance for Arthur Razor. That's his landlord."

During Chris and Nancy's marriage, a cellmate of Chris Smith's, named Tom Haskett, moved in with them. For a while, Haskett's wife, Debbie, also stayed there but after a time, Nancy said, "They moved out to another apartment that Razor owned for a while and then they moved back in with us and then he told her to go home to her folks and so then Tom was with us for a while by himself."

In November of 1990, Chris and Nancy had a falling out. She moved into a battered women's shelter in Muncie and filed for a divorce.

Nancy said, "I only knew of a few of Chris's friends." She had never heard him speak of Ralph Jacobs, Wolfman, or Crandall. "He never had friends over. He always stayed by my side because he's always afraid I was going to do something. He wouldn't even let me go to the store unless he was with me the whole time." She added, "We only got together with his family twice the whole time we were together."

The detectives asked Nancy about weapons and drugs. She told them that, "Chris had a couple of BB guns. He never carried a pistol. And neither of us ever used marijuana."

The baby became fussy during the interview. Baker and Shoemaker tried to distract him with toys but his mother said, "He doesn't get around many men because of his dad." Nancy said she had had no contact with Chris Smith since her divorce.

She had seen him once. "There was a passing where he was coming from court and I grabbed his kid and ran for the Sheriff's office over at the county jail. I was seeing Tom at the time." Nothing was said, she related, because, "I went into the office where he couldn't see us. I got in there before he even stepped into the building." The officers assured her that they would not release her contact information to Smith.

On May 29, 1992, Detective Shoemaker had Chris's brother, Tracy Dean Smith, retrieved from the Henry County Jail and brought over for questioning. Tracy stated that he lived at Qualls Trailer Court with his brother, Charles C. Smith, and Charles's wife, Connie.

Tracy recalled that on February 13, 1992, he spent the night at Chris's place and the next day they walked to Stonegate apartments where his estranged wife, Tina A. Smith, resided. They arrived around 1:00 p.m. and watched television until about 6:00 p.m.

Then they went to drink beer at the Twilight. They returned to Chris's apartment along with a pal named Jerry. Tracy did not know the man's last name.

Tracy borrowed Jerry's moped and went back to Stonegate to see if Tina had returned. She had not. The brothers returned to the Twilight where Chris got into a fight with some of his relatives. Shoemaker asked what the fight was about. Tracy told him that, "Terry Alton's brother, Bill Alton, had molested my niece."

Asked if Chris wanted to kill Alton, Tracy said no. "He just wanted to fight him." The people at the bar broke up the fight before anyone got hurt. Tracy, Chris, and Jerry were asked to leave. They returned to Chris's apartment around 1:00 a.m.

All three were drunk. Jerry took off sometime during the night and the brothers awoke around 8:00 a.m. Two hours later they again walked to Tina's apartment where they hung around for about an hour, and then they walked to their sister's house. They stayed for supper. Chris left around 6:00 p.m.

"I didn't see him again until Sunday, February 17th. That was after the murder. He came to Wyona's to get a bicycle from our sister's garage. Told us he'd been to Kentucky with Jim Gregory, doing a little work on Gregory's farm. Chris was never lazy. If there was work to be had, he'd do it."

Chris left on the bike and Tracy did not see his brother again until March, 1991. At that time, both brothers were in the Henry County Jail. There was a shakedown on March 9 and the brothers had a few moments to speak. "I asked Chris about the murder. I've asked him a couple of times and he denied that he shot Junior Crandall. He denied it. He said, 'I did not shoot him.'"

Sergeant Kim Cronk was also reinterviewed about Crandall's homicide. He answered all questions with the help of his report and his recollected answers were consistent with that report.

Baker and Shoemaker continued asking questions. Lester Hopkins had dinner at the Jacobs home the night of the murder but left before Stephens came. Wayne Daniels, Ralph's friend, confirmed that Ralph took pictures in bars and that he had spoken with Ralph and police during the investigation.

Another friend, Larry Alsip, had been on the phone with Ralph around 5:00 p.m. the evening of the murder. They talked about baseball cards and videotaping shows off the television. When Jacobs was in jail, he spoke with Alsip and asked him to obtain phone records for that day.

Robbie Barkley, who was friends with both Smith and Jacobs, described being at the Twilight with Chris when he heard about an incident on 18th Street. The two walked down to investigate. Baker and Shoemaker's report read: "Barkley and Smith went to the area of the police cars and went to Mr. Wood's residence. Stood on the front porch and watched. Was at Wood's house about forty-five minutes. Then each went home. Barkley said he'd never known Smith and Jacobs to run around together. Barkley said he did not know Crandall."

Charlie Alcorn admitted to police that he had robbed Crandall, and then retracted the story because he "received a lot of heat from the people on the street about ripping off Crandall." He responded by telling people that he had only admitted to the burglary to get out of jail. Then he again admitted to robbing Crandall and described some of Crandall's guns.

Wilma J. Davis, who had known Crandall for fourteen years, was questioned on June 4, 1992. She told Shoemaker and Baker that she had last seen Crandall a week prior to his death. She stated that Crandall told her that, "Charlie Alcorn and Gene Davis had ripped him off of $30,000 worth of marijuana." She related that Crandall also told her that on the day he was killed, "he was expecting a ten-pound shipment of marijuana."

Did Crandall know Smith or Jacobs? Just by sight, according to the investigators' report. "Wilma stated that she and Crandall observed Chris Smith walking down the street one day and Crandall asked her what was wrong with Smith's leg. Wilma told Crandall that his name was Chris Smith and he had cancer."

Officers telephoned James Gregory in Kentucky. His statements during this interview matched his taped statements in 1991. "Mr. Gregory stated that from the time he and Chris Smith left New Castle, arrived at his cabin and returned to New Castle the next day, him and Chris Smith was only apart from each other about ten minutes, when he left Chris at the cabin while he picked up supper."

The witness statements were cohesive. If Thompson wanted to go to court and try to point the finger at either Smith or Jacobs, he'd have a hard time proving it.

CHAPTER 17—THE BEAST

It was time to talk to Thompson about the Crandall murder. On June 5, 1992, Baker and Shoemaker went to the Marion County Jail to question their suspect. Thompson, brought from his cell, treated the investigators as if they were some small inconvenience.

Baker and Shoemaker started with basic questions. Did Thompson know their witnesses: Doug Percy, Bobby West, and David Loveless? Thompson was noncommittal. "Yeah, maybe."

What about the murder victim, Wesley Crandall? Thompson replied with a shrug. "Never heard of him." Hadn't he traveled to New Castle, Indiana, on the evening of the murder with Doug Percy? Hadn't they gone to Crandall's home? "Sure, I been to New Castle. Doug came with me and some other guys sometimes. But never just the two of us."

Thompson again denied knowing Wesley Crandall and acted as if the interview were over. If they were finished with their little cat-and-mouse game, he had things to do.

But the officers wanted to talk about David Loveless. "The way we heard it, Loveless introduced you to someone for a possible drug deal."

Thompson had his own version of the story. "Me, my brother David, and Doug Percy went with Loveless to a house to see about a pit bull. But I never went inside." Why not? Thompson grinned. "Me and Percy? Lemme tell ya. We was drunk. Couldn't find our way outta the truck."

Later, Thompson changed his story and said he might have gone inside the house.

Was there a shotgun? Yes, Jerry remembered a shotgun. "My girlfriend, Shawn McCormick, she bought a shotgun, must have been 16 or 20 gauge, at Kmart in New Castle." She had her paycheck and used that to purchase the gun. "It was a surprise to me. I was busy buying a couple of wristwatches."

The investigators showed Thompson a copy of the firearm purchase form signed by Shawn McCormick. Yes, Thompson told them, that was the gun she bought. "What happened to it?" Baker and Shoemaker asked.

Thompson said, "When we went back to Doug Percy's house where we were staying, Shawn gave me the gun. It was a nice piece and I was surprised, but I gave it to Doug Percy."

"You never fired the gun?" Shoemaker challenged.

Thompson admitted that he discharged the weapon a couple of times. "Then I gave it to Percy because having it would violate my probation. Percy, he took the shotgun to where he works and machined the barrel."

There was one other incident with the shotgun, Thompson recalled slowly. "Doug Percy ripped off Bobby West in a drug transaction. West showed up at Percy's house with a gun, trying to get Percy. When Bobby got to Percy's front door, I took the shotgun that Shawn had bought for me and shot Bobby's Chevette in the driver's door. Bobby heeded the warning and left." The officers scribbled notes without speaking and Thompson added, "That was before Percy cut down the shotgun."

Shoemaker leaned back. "Maybe you left some things out of your story about Bobby West's visit, big guy. Why don't you tell us again how that all happened?"

"It was just like I said," Thompson protested. He related the events again but then said, "I was merely defending myself. What would you do if someone was after you with a gun?"

Asked about the trip to Texas, Thompson said that was Percy's idea. "Doug, he wanted me to help him find a person he had posted bond for and who skipped out. Then, when we were stopped in Illinois, Doug was arrested for open container law and carrying guns without a permit. The guns were Percy's," Thompson declared. They could check the court records. They could check with the attorney. "Percy admitted both guns were his. I did not even know those guns were in the truck."

Percy owned several guns, Thompson said. He acquired them at a bar. He had a chrome revolver, a 9mm handgun, two Uzis, and a derringer. "The 9mm handgun and one of the Uzis were confiscated by Illinois State Police. The Derringer was sold or traded by Percy to a person named Stick. He's left the state."

Near the end of the interview, Thompson intoned that the truth would come out about the murder charges he was currently charged with. Baker and Shoemaker advised Jerry that they did not want to talk about the Marion County homicides.

They continued their discussion and then Thompson became intense and stiffened in his chair. "You're investigating the Wesley Crandall murder where Ralph Jacobs and Kiki Smith went to jail for?"

"We've been reinvestigating that homicide for a month," the investigators told him. "Now is your chance to tell your side of the story. The derringer has been recovered and Stick has been talked to."

Visibly upset, Thompson told the investigators that, "Doug killed the men in the car lot on his way to work. He told me all about it. I was not there." He added, "I might have been in Crandall's house a long time ago, but I don't know nothing about the killing."

His pickup was in the area, the officers nudged. "Wasn't my pickup," Thompson claimed. "I once had a Chevy pickup truck with a shell on it, but it was falling apart, didn't drive worth a darn. I might go a coupla blocks, but I wouldn't trust that old truck to make it to New Castle."

Was he sure about that? Had he possibly driven his Chevy truck to New Castle in February of 1991, and parked it in the 1800 block of F Avenue?

Thompson backed out of the interview, invoking his right to council.

As the investigators walked away, Thompson called out, "I got twenty guys who'll testify I was with them at the time of those car lot killings. Ask anybody!"

CHAPTER 18—PUTTING TOGETHER THE PUZZLE

Having conducted multiple interviews, Baker and Shoemaker met on June 23, 1992, at the Indianapolis Police Department to share information with Indianapolis Police Detectives Tom Minor and Dave Phillips. The officers exchanged reports about witnesses and guns. Jerry Thompson was now under a microscope.

Thompson's family members were interviewed by Baker and Shoemaker on June 24th and 25th. They met with his eldest brother, Tony Thompson, and Lori Fox. The couple said that on the day of Crandall's murder, Thompson and Percy had stopped at their residence at 401 South Walnut Street in New Castle. They explained that the three brothers, Tony, Jerry, and David had a fight on New Year's Eve and damaged the drywall. Jerry and Doug Percy had helped repair the damage and had come to pick up Percy's drywall tools.

Jerry's brother Steve lived in Indianapolis. He said that he and Jerry had not socialized lately and were "not on the best of terms." Steve said that Jerry was ruthless and had threatened him "on an occasion shortly after the incident with the stolen vehicles." He said Jerry would not have confided in him about any illegal activity.

When approached at his job, Jerry's brother David stood up for Jerry. He told the officers that, "When me, Jerry, Percy, and David Loveless went to that house in New Castle, it was not drug related. We were simply there to look at a dog. Jerry is too kind a person to ever kill anyone. Jerry's heart is too big to commit murder. Furthermore, I have never in my life seen Jerry with any kind of weapon in his hands."

Baker and Shoemaker's investigation had been thorough. When Henry County Prosecutor Malcolm K. Edwards filed his list of witnesses on October 14, 1992, he had fifty-two solid witnesses plus twenty-eight witnesses he could use but did not plan to call.

Thompson's best hope was to get out on bond.

Jerry Thompson's Defense Attorney Kit Crane arrived at Thompson's bond hearing prepared to argue for his client's freedom. "The unsubstantiated claims that the wrong men have been jailed for this murder is a feeble reason to incarcerate my client." His contention was that Jerry Thompson did not deserve to be in jail.

Kit Crane's first witness for the Defense was Jim Stephens. "I've been employed by the City of New Castle for twenty-three years and been a detective for twenty," he related. "I estimate that I've investigated hundreds, possibly thousands of crimes and been involved in 80 percent of the local murder investigations."

How many murder investigations? "About fifteen during my tenure," was Stephens's estimation. Listing his qualifications, Stephens said, "I had attended five different crime scene investigative schools before the Crandall murder."

"How many seminars have you attended for interrogation training?" Crane asked.

Stephens replied, "With death investigation there's usually a segment on interrogation. I have attended one school put on by the FBI in Delaware County at Ball State University just for interrogation but that was the only school for just that."

"Okay. I take it, sir, you are aware that there have been allegations raised that there were some threats and coercion against Christopher Smith and Ralph Jacobs Jr. prior to their cases. Is that correct?"

"Oh, I heard about it, alright," Stephens said. "Small town. It happens."

"Ever happen before?"

Stephens said, "The only other time such allegations were raised against me was during the previous murder of Tamera Weaver. The defendant in that case also raised allegations. But he was found guilty and nothing further happened in regard to those allegations."

He said that when he interviewed Jacobs there were "numerous interruptions" that required him to turn the tape off while taking the man's statement. "There were times during that interview that we spoke to the Prosecutor. There were times when other witnesses showed up. We would stop to give him a break; he wanted a coke, coffee, something of that nature." But when the tape was off, "I don't know that we had any conversation with him," Stephens said.

Only once, Stephens said, had they talked with Jacobs about the Crandall murder before taping his interview. "Once we had established that there was a reason to take a statement, then we turned the tape on." Jacobs had signed a Waiver of Rights-Advice of Rights form prior to each day's interview, Stephens pointed out.

There were two or three statements but one was recorded over. Stephens said, "It's my recollection that somehow the tape had been placed back in the tape machine so that Cronk could listen to what had been said and I failed to remove that tape and then taped over it again with Smith's." He thought that might have been the second tape.

"At any time, sir, did you tell Ralph Jacobs off the record what to say when the tape machine was then turned on?" Crane asked.

"Absolutely not."

"Did you ever tell Ralph Jacobs any of the particulars about this crime?"

"No, sir."

"At any time did you ever give Ralph Jacobs the name of Christopher Smith? How did the name Christopher Smith first come up in your conversations with Ralph Jacobs?" Crane wanted to know.

Stephens replied, "Well, the best I remember is that Ralph Jacobs brought it up." He hadn't shown Smith's photo to Jacobs, either, he said. "Sergeant Cronk handled about all the photo arrays and you'd have to ask him about that."

Stephens testified that both men signed waivers, stating that they understood their rights, neither asked for an attorney, and both gave statements voluntarily and of their own free will. And in fact, Christopher Smith had told Stephens that he could read and write, and that he lacked three months having his diploma. Jacobs also claimed to be literate.

"Did you have any doubt that they couldn't read?" Crane asked.

"No," Stephens insisted. "They told me they could, examined the Interrogation Advice of Rights and appeared to be reading it, and signed it."

"Did you have any doubts when you conducted the investigation of Wesley Crandall, based on your experience, that Christopher Smith and Ralph Jacobs murdered Wesley Crandall?" Crane asked.

"I did not."

Crane then asked Stephens specifically, "When Christopher Smith was released from Henry County Jail did you ever approach him on a sidewalk and threaten him? Since his release from incarceration?"

"No, sir," Stephens replied. "I've seen Chris Smith one time." It was someplace that sold antiques, he thought. "And I don't think he even knew that I saw him. That was just recently, like two or three weeks ago."

"You've heard the allegation that you drove up and saw him on the sidewalk and apparently threatened him?" Crane queried.

Stephens shook his head. "I have not spoke to Chris Smith or seen him other than what I've just described."

Crane dismissed Stephens and turned his attention to Mark Winchester. How had he had identified Smitty? Winchester said, "I passed him in the hallway at Crandall's house but at that time I did not know his given name, only his nickname, 'Smitty.'" He later picked his photograph from an array presented to him. Otherwise he was able to describe Crandall's two visitors only as a bigger and smaller guy.

"Do you see this gentleman sitting beside me?" Crane asked. "Have you ever seen him before?"

"No, I haven't," Winchester responded.

Crane said, "Just for the record, I would like to reflect that Jerry Thompson is sitting to my right. You've never seen him before?"

"No. I don't think so." He had identified Smitty as the smaller guy. He had told investigators that he was 90 percent certain that Smitty was the man he saw. Satisfied, Crane passed the witness to the prosecutor.

Prosecutor Malcolm Edwards asked Winchester if he had paid any attention to the larger man. His only observation was that he was "kind of a big guy with dark hair." Winchester said that was correct and Edwards asked, "Would you know the bigger guy again if you saw him?"

"No."

But in his earlier statements, Edwards reminded everyone, Winchester had said repeatedly that he thought the man was Smitty. "Is it fair," he asked, "to say that those responses would indicate that at that time you were something less than a hundred percent certain that it was Smitty?"

"Yes."

He had not seen either man clearly. "As I recall there weren't any lights on. It was kind of dingy."

"Well, do you have some doubt in your mind now, today?"

"Of course, I do. Because of the events that have transpired."

Kit Crane next questioned Ralph Jacobs's uncle, Levi Jacobs, about his relationship with his brother's family at the time of the Crandall death. Levi Jacobs had worked at Navistar in Indianapolis for twenty-two years. "I had a sleeping room on Ritter Avenue during the week and frequently stayed with Ralph's family on weekends. My work shift at the time was 4:00 p.m. to 12:30 a.m., Monday through Friday."

Crane was quick to highlight the discrepancy. "So, on a Thursday in February you would have been working for Navistar. Is that correct? Do you remember taking any days off from work in February, 1991?"

Levi did not recall.

"And how do you know you were at the house that night when he got arrested"

He had been in the garage with his brother, Ralph Sr., when Ralph Jr. carried wood for him and then went to the store. "And then they all went in the house. My brother came back out and told me. I mean, I wasn't present when he got arrested."

Crane asked if he had been drinking and Levi said, "I had a few beers."

Was it possible that Ralph could have gone somewhere that night without Levi knowing it? "You didn't sit on him that day?"

Levi said he could not say for certain that Ralph never left.

Crane next asked about Levi's guns. Levi told the Court, "I had only one shotgun, a 20 gauge, in the garage. That shotgun was locked up in the garage and no one could get it but me. No one else had a key."

Defense Attorney Crane's next witness was twenty-seven-year-old Shawn McCormick who lived at 1418 Deloss in Indianapolis. She had met Jerry Thompson in August or September of 1990. He had fathered her daughter, nine-month-old Jerri Nicole Thompson. "Me and Jerry moved in with Doug Percy in January, 1991. I left in July and I guess Jerry stayed there," she recalled.

She did remember buying a shotgun at Kmart on February 12, 1991. "I think, I think I told them it was a double barrel, but I believe it was a single barrel for hunting. I bought it for hunting."

She went with Thompson and Percy but could not remember who drove. "…but I do know that I had gotten off work and I work nights, so…" She paused and then said, "by the time I got off work I was purdy dazed for being so tired. More than likely Jerry [drove]) 'cause Doug was usually drunk so if we drove anywhere, probably it was Jerry."

Crane asked McCormick, "Did you ever come to New Castle with Doug and Jerry for purposes of some type of uh, drug deal or purchasing any drugs from some individual by the name of Bobby West or for that matter, from any individual in New Castle?" McCormick denied knowing who Bobby West was and Crane asked, "Do you know whether Bobby West ever gave any money, $600 or any other sum, to Jerry or Doug Percy?"

"No, I don't know nothing about $600," she told Crane. "My plan that day was to take Jerry's dad, Marvin, for an outing. My idea was to buy the shotgun and take Marvin hunting because he was really, really sick. I thought we could go rabbit hunting and he could do something; you know? Beside sit around and watch the cancer eat him?"

She couldn't say why she chose Kmart. "I don't even remember; we had just stopped and I happened to have the money at that time and I decided to go ahead and buy it."

On that trip two watches were purchased, one was given to McCormick and the other to Doug's wife, Jerra. McCormick had been paid that day and could not remember if Jerry gave her any money that day or not. "Any money that was accumulated between the two of us was always gave to me."

The last time she saw the shotgun was the day she bought it. She related, "When we got out of the truck, I was tired and I was going in to bed and Jerry and Doug went to the garage, and as far as I know that's where it went was to the garage." Later, "I seen a thing about this big." She gestured with her hands. "I asked them what it was and they said it was the handle, the butt of the shotgun. It was laying on the floor of the garage."

Crane again asked McCormick about Bobby West, who reportedly gave Thompson $600 shortly before the shotgun was purchased. McCormick insisted she did not know him. "I do remember Jerry meeting with two men at the gas station while I was working but I didn't know their names and I never heard what they talked about."

She also did not remember any incident of Jerry shooting the shotgun at a car. "Now, there was a time where it was supposed to have happened. I think Jerry said that he had shot at them guys 'cause they was coming up there starting a bunch of stuff and Doug's kids was there." She remembered nothing about the shooting except, "I know nobody was killed or anything, that's all I can tell you that I know."

After she moved out of Percy's house, Doug and his wife, Jerra, still called their former houseguest. McCormick said, "At one time Doug did ask me if he left his wife would me and my baby leave with him." That happened before charges were brought up on Thompson, she said.

"Let me ask you this," Crane said. "Did you ever have a relationship, other than being friends, with Doug Percy?"

"Oh no."

The only thing McCormick remembered about the day of the murder was that she and Thompson went down the street to Marsh Supermarket on Post Road and bought a

Valentine's Day cake. They had it decorated with her name, Jerry's, Doug's and Jerra's.

Crane asked McCormick about her current attorney, Carolyn Raider. "What charges are you currently facing in Marion County?"

She replied, "Yeah, uh, something about auto theft and uh, something about supposedly knowin' something 'cause I lived with him."

McCormick had been arrested and questioned multiple times. "And then I was arrested and questioned a couple of weeks before I delivered, they put me in jail and then when my baby was two months old, they arrested me, uh, and uh, then by the New Castle's [police] with my attorney present, this time." She insisted, "I don't know anything about this."

Prosecutor Malcolm Edwards questioned McCormick next and asked for specifics about the time of the murder. She recalled that when she worked at the station, Thompson came in with some friends. He had taken some pills, possibly Vivarin, from the store. "Just a bottle of them. I used to take them to stay awake to go to work." McCormick said she paid for anything she took from the store but was vague about Thompson's pills.

What she recalled about her visit to New Castle on February 12, 1991, was, "I think these guys went down there to see somebody. We went to an apartment somewhere. Whoever it was, I think it was the guy that was at the gas station. I think his name might have been Bobby, but I met the man only briefly and I saw hundreds of people a day during my shift. Doug and Jerry knocked on a door but there was no answer."

Prosecutor Edwards asked about Jerry crushing some pills. McCormick could not remember seeing them specifically. Edwards said, "I'm just asking you under oath, now, to the best of your recollection, did he take anything, any part of those pills, or any powder from those pills to New Castle that day?"

She wasn't sure.

Edwards continued to drill her for details.

When they went into Kmart, McCormick said, she had no intention of buying a shotgun. She looked at fishing equipment first. Then she decided to impress Marvin with a shotgun. She had used a 20 gauge when hunting with her husband but asked the clerk which shotgun was the best. The clerk selected the gun for her, she said, and picked out the shells.

"Did you know at that time whether or not Jerry was allowed to possess a shotgun?" Edwards asked her.

"Now, see, that's something I'm not clear on. Because I was always under the impression that a shotgun was not illegal. I know handguns are, but I did not know a shotgun was illegal to have in your house, or for the purpose of huntin'. Even what my husband told me is when you've got a shotgun and you're going huntin' the gun's gotta be in one part of the car and the shells in another part."

McCormick had been told that Thompson was a convicted felon but she had never asked what crimes he had committed. "When I gave Jerry the gun, he didn't act all that thrilled. He was like, 'I'm going to give this to Doug.' And, at first there was a little conversation about you know, why, I just bought this, but he said look, we're living here with them, we're giving Jerra a watch, you know, let's be nice."

"I did not actually give Jerry the gun," she said. "It was just carried out of the truck. Jerry carried it out of the truck."

"But, after you got back from Indianapolis with this gun that you had bought to go hunting with Marvin and to impress Marvin, you never saw it again?" Edwards asked her.

"No, I was told they prefer not to have a gun in the house because of the kids." She never went hunting with Marvin. McCormick said again that on the day that Thompson reportedly shot at the Chevette, she did not remember what she heard, only what was said afterward, "Something about

Doug and his family being there, the kids being there and this guy coming over and keeps calling, keeps going around the house and stuff like that, that's all I remember."

She had told Mr. Crane that no one got killed, Edwards reminded her. "Did you know whether anyone got hurt?"

"I have no idea," McCormick responded. "Like I said, I don't even remember this happening."

In redirect, Kit Crane asked McCormick, "Do you recall some evening when Doug accused Jerry of molesting one of their daughters?"

"Yeah. This wasn't brought up until after we had split up. I heard something about that." She only recalled that Percy and Thompson had been out drinking and had picked her up. She was with Thompson that night. "Doug never said anything, Jerry never said anything and then the next day, I think it was Jerry said, 'I can't believe Doug said that.'"

Crane wanted to know, what was McCormick's background?

She left her husband, Joe McCormick, about six months before she met Jerry, but she and Joe were currently still married. Joe worked at a sheet metal company called Willoughby's in Indianapolis.

Winding up the bond hearing, Kit Crane addressed the Court, saying, "This is a case where two individuals have already entered this Courtroom, pleaded guilty, were sentenced by this Court for this offense." They had changed their stories only after Captain Baker and Detective Shoemaker approached them with an offer to help. Jacobs, he said, kept remembering more and more things that Stephens supposedly told him. "Mr. Jacobs knew quite a bit about the specifics about that murder scene that he denied Jim Stephens telling him until after he gave this statement and then he, Mr. Jacobs would testify, 'Oh, yeah, Jim Stephens told me that too.'"

Percy had contradicted himself, Crane alleged. "Bobby West doesn't recall making any of the statements that he earlier made to Detective Baker and Detective Shoemaker. Shawn remembered little of the incidents except for a Valentine's Day cake. Percy was unable to provide any directions to places he'd supposedly been and the two-hour drive was never recorded.

"I believe Detective Baker or Shoemaker, one of them, testified that they drove past the victim's house no less than eight times before Mr. Percy was able to point that house out as being the house that he was at supposedly with Jerry Thompson when Mr. Crandall was murdered.

"It just appears to me that there is not a strong presumption of guilt and that the proof of guilt toward Jerry Thompson was not great at this bond hearing. I think everything considered, that Mr. Thompson is deserving that bail be set in this matter." Crane thanked the court and Malcolm Edwards rose to his feet.

The Defense had proved nothing, Edwards challenged. "The case essentially rests upon initially the testimony of Mr. Percy. Which has not been effectively contradicted in any way, including no presentation of what might amount to an alibi." He pointed out that depositions had been given, although some witnesses suffered memory lapse on the stand. There was the evidence of the recovered weapons. Much evidence corroborated Mr. Percy's statements "and there is no evidence in this record to significantly contradict that evidence and it's my contention, Your Honor, the defendant has simply not met the burden that is required of him in this case and should not be let to bail."

While the Court debated whether or not to release Thompson on bail, a previous Motion, requesting that Thompson be held in the Henry County Jail through the next afternoon while recently acquired evidence was examined had not been ruled on. The Court's ruling was that the sheriff was to be alerted, and that Crane's interview with Thompson would take place at the jail. "In talking with the sheriff, he expressed his concern about the manpower it would take to provide security for Mr. Thompson if he were, in fact, at your private office."

***

On December 30, 1992, Judge Tom McNichols granted Jerry K. Thompson's petition for bail—at $250,000. This came as a surprise to prosecutors because according to Indiana State Law, "murder is not bailable when the proof is evident or the presumption strong."

Henry County Prosecutor Malcolm Edwards said the decision was moot since Thompson was being held in the Marion County Jail—without bond—accused of four other murders.

"So, he's not going anywhere," Edwards said.

CHAPTER 19—DOUGLAS PERCY: STAR WITNESS

Jerry Thompson was brought to trial for Wesley Crandall's murder. In preparation, New Castle investigators set to work tying a noose around their case. They re-questioned witnesses and documented Thompson's background. The excavation of Percy's property had given them viable pieces of the murder weapon.

Following the trail of Crandall's stolen guns, Captain Butch Baker contacted Jeff Vaughn of Jeff's Guns. Mr. Vaughn was able to produce a record, which showed that Wesley W. Crandall, 1218 South 18th Street, had purchased a 9mm, M-11 from him on October 9, 1990. Mr. Vaughn brought all of the guns' purchase ledgers for the gun shop with him to meet with Baker. Together, they checked records up to February 14, 1991.

From October 9, 1990, to December 16, 1990, Crandall purchased three 9mm guns: an SWD M11, a Charter Arms Pit Bull, and a Stallard. He also purchased three .22s: a Davis Derringer, and two Jennings, plus a Taurus 357. Investigators had recovered a .22 caliber Davis Derringer and a 9mm Stallard JS9M. They were able to raise partial serial numbers from the derringer but none from the Stallard. They did have Doug Percy's testimony that the guns, including the Stallard, had been taken from Wesley Crandall's apartment.

***

On July 13, 1992, Carolyn Radar received a letter from the Marion County Prosecutor's Office offering immunity to Shawn L. McCormick in exchange for her testimony. The letter from Prosecutor Malcolm K. Edwards referenced a call from Captain Baker of the New Castle Police Department and read in part:

"It is my understanding that your client, Shawn L. McCormick, is willing to give the State of Indiana any information she possesses related to the shooting death of Wesley Crandall Jr., in New Castle on February 14, 1991.

"In return, on the basis of the following conditions, the State agrees to extend use immunity and derivative use immunity to Ms. McCormick, whereby any information that she provides concerning the homicide in question or evidence that she gives concerning the homicide in question or evidence derived from that information or evidence, may not be used in any criminal proceedings against her, other than in a prosecution for perjury. The conditions referred to above are as follows:

1) She was not present when Crandall was killed;

2) The information she gives will be true, complete, and accurate to the best of her knowledge and belief;

3) She will give the State full cooperation in the investigation of this matter and will testify truthfully whenever required by the State; and

4) She will submit to polygraph and/or voice stress examinations concerning this matter as requested.

"If any of these conditions are not met, this extension of immunity is void."

Shawn McCormick and her attorney agreed to these terms.

At the trial, McCormick's testimony was that she met Jerry Thompson in the fall of 1990 and shortly afterward the couple moved into the Percy home. She worked at the Shell station at 21st Street and Post Road. She purchased a shotgun at the New Castle, Indiana, Kmart on February 12, 1991, using her own money. Percy and Thompson were in the store at the time.

McCormick stated that she purchased the gun and ammunition to hunt rabbits. She described her purchase as a shotgun that held two rounds of ammunition, "You know, the kind with the little BB's in them."

When she returned to the Percy home in Indianapolis, Jerry Thompson carried the shotgun into the garage. She never saw it again. About two weeks later, she believed she saw the stock of the gun.

***

During the hearing, Thompson's defense attorney, Kit Crane, summoned David D. Cashdollar, an investigator for the Indiana State Police. He had been with the State Police since September 1, 1966. He was a latent fingerprint examiner and certified by the National Association for Identification. His credentials included a degree in Criminal Justice from Indiana University and a Master's Degree from Ball State University. He testified that he participated in the investigation of the murder of Wesley Crandall, "in the collection and documentation and preservation of physical evidence at the scene."

On the night of Crandall's murder, Cashdollar arrived at the crime scene at the same time as the coroner, Bill Palmer. Other officers were already on the scene. He found the dwelling in serious disarray. The stench of dog feces and urine assaulted him immediately, although no dogs were visible. He understood that the animals were locked in the basement.

When Cashdollar arrived in the kitchen, a pillow with a Garfield pillowcase lay north of the victim's body on a stack of newspapers, which lay atop a cardboard barrel. His best recollection was that Deputy Bill Fox assisted him in measuring items and their locations for the still photographs.

"Do you know how many photographs you took that night?" Crane asked. "Did any photos that were taken at the scene later come up missing?"

"Not to my knowledge," Cashdollar responded. He did not recall counting the photographs but, "The negatives should be filed at Connersville State Police Post."

Items collected were numbered and listed on control sheets. Referring to sixteen items collected at the Crandall murder scene, Crane asked Cashdollar if, "it would be your testimony that those items, those sixteen items, have been destroyed?"

Cashdollar responded, "The best of my recollection is that these items listed were either released to someone or destroyed at a later time." Some of the items were firearms and others "would have been released to whomever was in charge of the victim's estate." He added, "I believe the rationale was the case had been disposed of at the time."

He could not be more specific because various departments "have policies that determine how long evidence will be held...or disposed of depending on the type of evidence whether it is contraband or firearms or evidence from a crime scene."

At the State Police level, Cashdollar said, "someone in a position to make that determination" would decide when evidence should be disposed of but it is all photographed, "either at the crime scene or afterwards."

Crane asked about the search warrant served on Douglas Percy's house. Cashdollar was present during the search and used a metal detector around the garage. "Was that search videotaped in any manner?" Crane asked.

Cashdollar responded that although video was becoming more common, he used still photography that day. All officers present began their search at the same time. An area twelve feet by eighteen feet in front of the garage was excavated. Douglas Percy pointed out items to investigators: a silencer, a nylon strap, and a burning barrel where officers discovered a black rubber Charter Arms pistol grip. Gun shells were also collected with Percy's help.

Crane wanted to know, "Was there any item of evidence recovered from the execution of that search warrant that was not pointed out by Douglas Percy?" Cashdollar was not sure. "Did Mr. Percy say anything to you while you were executing this search warrant?"

Cashdollar replied that, "he was explaining the excavation of what he referred to as the gun shelves in the garage in my presence."

"Did Douglas Percy say anything to you or direct you in any other direction or any other manner other than his explanation of this cavity in the block wall in the back of the garage?"

Cashdollar did recall that Percy was, "talking about an individual who had cut up guns and driven thin sections of gun barrels, etc., into the driveway area where we were excavating." There may have also been some isolated digging around the burn barrel, he noted. No fingerprints were collected during the search.

CHAPTER 20—A MURDERER STANDS TRIAL

Crandall's neighbor, Gladys Case, still insisted that the man she had seen the night of the murder was Wolfman. But shown photos, she was amazed at the resemblance between Ralph Jacobs and Douglas Percy. Winchester testified that the man he saw with Smitty that night was bigger than Smitty.

When questioned by Defense Attorney Kit Crane, Christopher Smith could not identify Jerry Thompson. Crane asked Smith about the statement he gave to the New Castle Police Department on February 17, 1991.

"I didn't give a statement," Smith replied. "I told him what he wanted to hear 'cause he threatened me." Who threatened him? "Jim Stephens." Smith told the Court that Sergeant Kim Cronk was present when it happened. No one else was present, Smith stated. "They wasn't nobody when they took me back there."

"How did Detective Stephens threaten you?" Crane asked.

"He told me if I didn't tell him what he wanted to hear, he was going to go and get, arrest my sister and take her kids to the Welfare Department." He explained, "When I first gave him a statement, I told him where I was at and everything. He told me I was a' lying 'cause he had a witness that would put me there on the scene."

When he was asked about the murder, Smith told them he knew nothing about it. "Then they asked me could they have, would I sign to let them go down an' search my place. I let them go search my place 'cause I didn't have nothing to hide."

Crane asked, "Did Detective Cronk ever threaten you in any way? Okay, did Detective Cronk ever browbeat you in any way?"

"No."

"Let me ask you this," Crane said, "when somebody says browbeat or browbeaten, what does that mean to you?"

"I do not know."

Did he know what the word "harassed" meant?

Yes. "When they're in there coaching you what to say and everything and threatening you." The word "threaten" meant, "When they tell you what they're going to do and threaten you then they don't do it." Smith said Cronk never harassed or threatened him.

Stephens never hit him or threw anything at him, he admitted, "but he was sitting there tappin' a pencil on the desk when he was talking to me, shutting the tape player off and on." At one point, Stephens had been trying to get Smith to say things that were not true. Then he left the room for about ten minutes, leaving Smith alone with Cronk. When that happened, "Kim Cronk didn't say a word to me," Smith recalled.

"But did you ever ask Kim Cronk to help you?"

"No, it didn't pass my mind."

Smith declared that Stephens had given him all the particulars of the Crandall murder: the position of the body, the fact that a pillow was used, and that the victim was shot in the head with a shotgun. Crane read Smith's statement to him line by line, asking if he remembered being asked those questions and making those statements. Smith did not. He did not remember his responses to earlier questions, only that he had said what he was told to say. "It's been nineteen…"

He paused, thinking, "almost two years and I try to wipe it all out of my mind."

Crane asked him, "Have you had an opportunity in the last nineteen months to read any of your statements that you gave?"

"I can't read or write." He said Attorney David Whitton had read the statements to him before he was sentenced. He remembered little of his statement except that he had sold a 20 gauge shotgun to Lillian Foster. He said he remembered that detail only because it actually happened.

Crane asked Smith if he ever told his attorney, David Whitton, that he was being threatened. Smith replied that he was afraid to tell his attorney because Stephens was there in the courtroom and he would go after Smith's sister and her children.

He did remember the plea agreement for thirty-eight years. "Dave Whitton told me, he goes, uh go, he says plead guilty to it. He said they got Ralph Jacobs going in to appear in Court against you and that he gone finger you." Smith's response? "I told Whitton I didn't do it. But I'll take it 'cause I was thinking back about my sister and my niece and nephew."

He also expected that if his case went to a jury, he would get sixty years. Whitton had told him he could expect thirty to sixty. Smith also never told his sister about the threats.

Still trying to excise an acknowledgement of guilt from Smith that would exonerate Thompson, Crane asked, "When you were in court that day pleading guilty to a murder that you now say you didn't commit, facing thirty-eight years in prison, why didn't you just look to the Judge and say, I need help, Detective Stephens has threatened me. Why didn't you say that?"

"'Cause Jim Stephens was sitting in there."

"Threatening you?" Crane challenged. "Tapping a pencil? Maybe saying something that alarmed you?"

"No." But Smith said he was still afraid to speak.

"If Detective Stephens wasn't sitting over there, would you have asked the Judge for help?"

"Yes."

But Stephens was not at the jail, Crane reasoned, and yet Smith had not contacted his attorney? He had not "asked Mr. Whitton to tell the Judge that you were being threatened?"

"No, 'cause Dave Whitton wouldn't take no collect calls." Beside that, Stephens had a reputation, Smith alleged. "I know how dirty Jim Stephens is. I seen him do it to other people. A bunch of people." He could not cite specific names.

During his months of incarceration, Smith continued his silence to protect his sister. "'Cause I been through it before. Welfare coming in and taking my brother and sister away from me." This happened, he said, when he was nineteen.

Smith testified that when Baker and Shoemaker, as a part of the new investigation, conducted taped audio and video interviews with him in prison, they said nothing to him before the tapes began nor after they were turned off.

After that interview, Dave Whitton came to Pendleton Reformatory with forms for Post-Conviction Relief. This had happened on May 26, 1992. Crane acted incredulous. "So, for roughly four months from the date that this Court sentenced you for this murder until the date that the detectives came and talked to you, for that four months, what did you do to try to get your conviction set aside if anything? Did you ever call and tell anybody or write letters or have letters written for you about what Detective Stephens did?"

No. He had done nothing. "But all the way, all the way through the whole thing, I denied everything." Except when he spoke on the tape machine or in court, Crane pointed out.

Since his release, Smith had hired Attorney David Neal. "Has David Neal taken steps to start a lawsuit against the City, the County, and the State for what you say they've done to you?" Crane asked. "Do you know how much money you're trying to gain from this lawsuit?"

"What the paper says," Smith responded. "Fifty-one million." He deserved the money, he told Crane. "They took nineteen months of my life and nineteen months away from my son."

Crane turned the witness over to Prosecutor Malcolm Edwards, who asked Smith if there had been any other motive behind his guilty plea. Smith told him that, at the time, he was trying to get out of the Henry County Jail and be sent to some other institution. He claimed that in the county jail, he was as badly treated as a stray animal. He said the facility was disgusting, due mainly to poor plumbing.

In redirect, Crane asked Smith about his memory loss. Smith replied, "I got a disease they call neurofibromatosis, it's a other thing, they call it Elephant Leg." It frequently affected his memory, including the present day in court.

"Did you ever think while this was going on," Crane asked, "to talk to the Henry County Welfare Department and ask them if Jim Stephens had any influence, not giving your name but just ask them if there was any influence that Jim Stephens had over the Welfare Department? In fact, do you have any knowledge that Jim Stephens has any influence over the Welfare Department?"

"I do not know."

Next, Kit Crane called Tracy Smith, age twenty-nine. Tracy validated that he had been with his brother, Chris, most of the day before and the day of the murder.

Crane had failed to re-establish Jacobs and Smith as possible killers. With this alibi gone, he launched into Thompson's defense. The entire Crandall murder trial seemed to be a recitation of preliminaries until the fifth day when Douglas Percy took the stand.

There was no wiggle room for the Defense in Percy's recitation of the events leading up to and following after the murder. Percy's testimony, coupled with the evidence from the crime scene and Crandall's stolen guns, left the jury with no doubt that Jerry Thompson had murdered Wesley Crandall.

Thompson was found guilty as charged with the murder of Wesley Crandall. Court records stated, "The jury determined that Jerry Thompson knowingly killed another human being, Wesley Crandall Jr., by shooting at and against the body of Wesley Crandall Jr. with a gun thereby inflicting a mortal wound upon Wesley Crandall Jr., causing him to die."

Thompson received a sixty-year sentence for the murder and an additional thirty years on a Habitual Offender sentencing enhancement.

CHAPTER 21—PREPARING TO FACE A KILLER

With Thompson behind bars for the murder of Wesley Crandall, the Marion County Prosecutor's Office turned their attention to the Indianapolis murders. Thompson's case was assigned to deputy prosecutors Larry Sells and John Commons. The evidence in the shooting deaths of Allen White and Kathy Boggs was mostly circumstantial, so the prosecutors decided to focus on the stronger case involving the Hillis Automotive murders of Melvin Hillis and Robert Beeler. The State intended to seek the death penalty.

Thompson was brought to Marion Superior Court, Criminal Division Room Three, for his initial hearing, or arraignment, on the murder charges. At that hearing he was represented by a court-appointed, part-time public defender, David Martenet. Diminutive, Martenet stood five feet, six inches, and barely weighed 150 pounds. Sells noted that the man failed to wear a tie in the courtroom.

Sheriff's deputies advised Martenet that Thompson was a very dangerous convicted killer who hated lawyers. They suggested that the attorney keep as much distance between Thompson and himself as the defense table would allow while the judge read the charges and explained Thompson's rights to him.

Martenet thanked the deputies for the advice, and then cringed when they escorted Thompson into the courtroom and seated the giant at the defense table a breath away from him.

Already sitting at the far end of the table, Martenet plastered his thigh against the table leg. Then Thompson inched his chair closer to the attorney's. The courtroom stood to honor the Judge's arrival. When invited to be seated, Thompson thumped his chair a little closer to Martenet's. The attorney's face went pale. He looked to the deputies for help, but they appeared to be focused on the Judge's words.

As the hearing progressed, Thompson continued to move in on Martenet, edging so close that the smaller man feared to breathe wrong. By the end of the hearing, Martenet was making desperate signals to the officers, but they merely smiled politely at him.

Finally, the hearing ended and Thompson left the courtroom under armed guard.

The deputies, returning to the courtroom, were confronted by a red-faced, visibly shaken Martenet. "Why in the hell did you let that monster get so close? He was right on me!"

Martenet fumed when the officers burst into laughter. "Well," one of them finally admitted, "we told Thompson that you are very hard of hearing, and that he would have to sit very close if he wanted his attorney to hear what he said."

A few days after the arraignment, the State filed its formal request for the death penalty. Martenet was released from the case; the Court had a responsibility to assign other, more experienced attorneys who were not part of the Court's regular public defender staff to defend Thompson's life.

Death penalty cases are rare because they require a substantial investment in time and resources. Although prosecutors are on a salary, defense attorneys charge a higher rate for death penalty cases and invest long hours in investigation and preparation of their defense—they take their time. They may interview and summon long lists of potential witnesses, dragging the trial date forward for years.

The Hillis Auto Sales murders did not come to trial in Marion County, Indiana, until 1996. Deputy Prosecutors Sells and Commons had obtained all the records from the trial of the murder of Wesley Crandall and the evidence of Crandall's stolen gun being used to kill Robert Beeler and Melvin Hillis. Photographs of the two men, gunned down without warning or provocation, churned Sells's stomach.

He forgot about food or sleep as he memorized every gruesome detail in each photograph, file, and evidence bag.

The murder weapon looked wicked. It sickened Sells to imagine the horror of the two men looking at their own doom screaming from the mouth of the heavy black barrel. But he was glad to have it. The gun would help point Jerry Thompson to a cell on Death Row where he belonged.

Thompson denied all charges and told the press that he "was not present and took no part in the incident at Hillis Auto Sales involving Melvin Hillis and Robert Beeler."

Sells determined to prove that was a lie. With or without attorneys, Thompson was a powerful foe and Sells believed in knowing his enemy. He learned everything he could about Thompson's life.

Jerry was the youngest of five siblings; he had three brothers and a sister. Sells considered the horror of the man's childhood, his truancy, and his struggles in school. Drugs and alcohol had impacted Thompson's behavior from an early age.

Thompson's father, Marvin Thompson, had died of cancer at age sixty-five on October 30, 1992. It did not appear that the father taught his children any respect for the law.

Records from the New Castle Police Department and the Henry County Sheriff's Department revealed an extensive criminal history for Marvin Thompson, dating back to the 1950s and comprised of seventy-two offenses. According to the Indiana Department of Correction, Marvin's file was destroyed in early 1990.

During Marvin's incarcerations, his wife, Sara, used the children to smuggle contraband in to her husband. Now retired and living in New Castle on Social Security, Sara was ill with leukemia and rheumatoid arthritis.

It appeared that Thompson's criminal record would match his father's if he also lived until his late sixties. In addition to seven juvenile referrals and five months served at the Indiana Boys' School at age sixteen, Thompson had racked up eighteen adult arrests, including six misdemeanor convictions and seven felony convictions.

In total, Thompson had spent nine of his past eleven years in jail or prison. During his various periods of incarceration in the Department of Corrections, Thompson received write-ups for:

Fighting
Possession of Gambling Paraphernalia
Lying to Staff
Tattooing or Self-Mutilation
Breaking Deadlock (no recreation, phone privileges, or visitation), three times
Possession of Property of Another
Possession of Intoxicant
Possession of Unauthorized Property
Unauthorized Possession of State Property, twice
Code 107 Possession of a Deadly Weapon
Disorderly Conduct
Possession of Drug Paraphernalia
Refusing a Drug or Alcohol Test
Refusing to Work or Accept Assignment

He had been in some fights too. One report read, "The defendant reported that while incarcerated at Westville, he was involved in an altercation in which he was protecting a younger inmate when he was attacked and stabbed two times in the back with an ice pick by another inmate. Further, the defendant stated while incarcerated at the Indiana State Farm, he was hit with a pipe that resulted in a facial scar.

Additionally, he stated he was involved in an altercation in which he was hit with a brick while incarcerated at the Pendleton Reformatory."

The jury never heard about Thompson's criminal past. The law would not allow it.

The defendant's work history appeared flimsy and scattered. Many of his jobs were interrupted by arrests.

In 1978, Thompson worked at a New Castle Taco Bell, earning $2.65 per hour. After three weeks he left to take another job at the Washington Park Cemetery as a maintenance worker and backhoe operator. This summer job also paid Thompson $2.65 an hour.

In 1979, Thompson went to work for J&S Remodeling, earning $5.50 per hour as a roofer and panel installer. He lost the job when he was arrested.

Indiana State Hospital in New Castle was Thompson's next job. He was a general maintenance worker and custodian. He also did grounds work. But the job ended after six months when he was again arrested.

Then, in 1984, Thompson worked on a factory line assembling motorcycles for Kawasaki Limited in Lincoln, Nebraska. He liked the work but after four months, he returned to Indiana due to his mother's illness.

He worked as a machine operator for Circle City Machine in 1988. He held that job for four months, and then was again arrested.

Thompson's most recent job had been five years previously. In 1991, he was a bartender at The Hustler Tavern, earning $300 per week. After six months, he had a falling out with the owner. His employment was terminated by mutual agreement.

At age thirty-four, Jerry Thompson had accumulated a work history of fewer than twenty-four months.

Sells read and reread every file, every interview, and still the facts did not add up. Horribly abused children often choose to become compassionate adults. And Jerry's siblings appeared to be gainfully employed and had left no trails of blood. His sister, Susan, was a nurse, a woman committed to taking care of others.

During his career, Sells faced down and convicted seventy killers in the courtroom. Some killed for money or jealousy or anger. None exhibited the brutality and the rage that emanated from Jerry Thompson. Thompson had no regard—none—for his fellow man.

When he and his defense attorneys had to meet with the prosecution team, Thompson glowered at Sells and Commons like an enraged beast. Clearly, he was used to seeing men cower when he growled. He wore his reputation for violence proudly, like a medal. Even in shackles, he displayed his disdain for the mere mortals who threatened to conquer him in court.

If he spent his lifetime in prison, Thompson could have decades to mangle the bodies and devour the souls of those luckless enough to be incarcerated with him. There would be no justice for his crimes until he lay dead. Sells determined that he would settle for nothing less than the death penalty. "Thompson's reign of terror must come to an end," he said.

***

Sells's first step in prosecuting Thompson was to reinterview and obtain a current statement from Doug Percy, a complete account of Percy's dealings with the killer, and to prepare him for an upcoming deposition to be taken by Thompson's attorneys. From his first statement offered on March 18, 1992, Doug Percy had been questioned a multitude of times, in and out of the courtroom. His testimony had never wavered in four years.

Thompson's accuser answered the summons and found himself surrounded by hard-hitting attorneys. Sells represented the State of Indiana. Defense attorneys representing Jerry Thompson were Robert V. Clutter, attorney with Brown, Hastings & Clutter, and also Jeffrey A. Baldwin with Van Treese, Dakich, Baldwin & Earnest.

Before Baldwin began to question him, Percy asked for something in writing, guaranteeing that he still had immunity. He was not satisfied until Sells assured him that the immunity extended to him before he gave his initial statement on March 18, 1992, was still in effect.

Jeffery Baldwin questioned Percy about being stopped and arrested in Illinois. "Where did you get the guns that were in the van?" Baldwin asked. The question, a simple one, was delivered with the force of a tiger's pounce.

Percy did not flinch. "Jerry acquired them from Wesley Crandall."

Between the time of Crandall's death on February 14, 1991, and the traffic stop on June 6, 1991, the 9mm pistol and the M-11 stolen from Crandall's apartment had traveled from Percy's garage to Thompson's Cadillac El Dorado and had eventually been placed in the van by Thompson. The guns were with them when they made the drive to Houston in search of David Van Horn.

"It was your decision to break the law rather than have Jerry not go with you?" Baldwin challenged. "You are saying Jerry insisted on taking the guns? And rather than drive it by yourself, you decided to break the law?"

Yes, he did break the law, Percy admitted. Plus, his trip was fruitless. Van Horn had managed to evade him and he came home with neither his bail money nor the fugitive. He didn't like knowing that the guns were in the van, "But who was I to tell Jerry no?" he asked.

Sells saw immediately that he could convince a jury that Percy, who was five feet ten and weighed approximately 150 pounds, was intimidated by Thompson.

Baldwin continued to question Percy's story, pacing up and down the timeline of events, looking for a soft spot he could claw open. Percy answered the defense attorney's questions calmly. He made no effort to disguise his own role in the murders. His statements had not changed since he first reported the murders in 1992. He would be a credible witness.

Sells said, "You were asked about the murders of Hillis and Beeler. You were asked about a car lot. I want to direct your attention to March 14 of 1991. Can you tell us whether or not on that date you went to Hillis Auto Sales on Brookville Road?"

He had, with Jerry Thompson. "I witnessed a double homicide. Jerry killed the men using a nine-millimeter gun—pistol." It was one of the guns taken from the van by State Troopers when he and Thompson were stopped in Illinois.

Sells asked, "Did you see Jerry Thompson take anything from the car lot or from Mr. Hillis or Mr. Beeler when he shot them on March 14, 1991?"

Percy replied that Thompson took wallets "and something that holds keys." He took the items from the men, tossed them onto the floor and told Percy to pick them up. He did.

Sells asked about the murders of Allen White and Kathy Boggs on La Salle Street in September of 1991. Percy replied that Thompson told him he had murdered the pair a day or two after it happened.

Sells handed Percy a photograph, which Percy identified as Jerry Thompson. "Does that photograph, marked Exhibit A, show the same Jerry Thompson that you testified about in these proceedings concerning the murder of Wesley Crandall on February 14, 1991, and the murders of Mr. Hillis and Mr. Beeler on March 14, 1991, and the murder of Kathy Boggs and Allen White in September of 1991?" Sells asked.

Percy responded that it was and Sells asked him, "All other events related to Jerry Thompson that you have testified about, that is the same person, the one portrayed in Exhibit A?"

With Percy's affirmative answer, Sells stood up. He was ready to fight. And if Percy was killed, or otherwise became unavailable to appear and testify at the trial of Jerry Thompson, the deposition taken that day could be presented at the trial in his stead. That was why Sells made certain that Percy identified Jerry Thompson through his photograph as the killer of Melvin Hillis and Robert Beeler.

CHAPTER 22—THE BATTLE BEGINS

Thompson's trial was held in the Marion Superior Court with Judge John R. Barney Jr. presiding. Judge Barney was an experienced, well liked and respected jurist who had conducted several death-penalty trials. He was a former prosecutor who knew the law and applied it fairly to all parties.

Larry Sells's strategy was to select for the prosecution the table closest to the jury. He wanted their eyes on him as much as possible. He also wanted them to have to look past him to see Thompson. No matter how well his lawyers dressed their client, Thompson would look slovenly. Sells made certain that he himself looked sharp. From his freshly clipped hair to the military high polish on his shoes, he was immaculate. His suits, always perfectly pressed, accentuated his six-foot-three height.

He chose a conservative power tie for the trial, bright red and blue stripes that drew viewers' eyes to his face. He reserved his favorite tie for final arguments. During those arguments, he wore an eye-catching patriotic tie depicting Old Glory. The tie, with its faded white background, paid homage to the Founding Fathers. It looked like a piece of history in blood red, navy, and copper colors emblazoned with the American flag and the words, "We the People…" from the Preamble of the United States Constitution.

Each time that Thompson caught Sells's eye, he glared. To show the killer that he was not intimidated, Sells frequently strolled past the Beast like John Wayne stepping over a prairie dog. He remained calm and erect, moving within inches of Thompson's grasp. He wanted the criminal to see him as a man walking freely and towering over him. He wanted Thompson to know he would never back down. In response to the killer's muttered threats, Sells eyed him as if he were no more remarkable than an empty chair. No one would ever again take the Beast's menacing looks seriously.

In reality, Sells was glad for the team of six armed deputies in the courtroom. While he remained aloof, refusing to show fear, common sense told him that given the chance, Thompson would devour him like raw hamburger. He was brave but not stupid.

Doug Percy also came under Thompson's evil eye. But Thompson's little friend wasn't buckling, not this time. Sells had warned him that the killer would try to terrify him, scare him out of telling the truth.

When Percy stepped to the witness stand to testify against Jerry Thompson, he was forced to brave the daggers of Thompson's wrath. There were murderous looks and muttered threats. Percy was clearly frightened of the bigger man, but his courage held. He answered questions directly and made no effort to excuse himself for his part in the events.

Sells stood between Percy and Thompson. He did not want Percy to even look at Thompson except to point his finger and say to the jury, "Yes, that's the man. He's the killer."

Sells questioned Percy at length, eliciting every terrifying and gory detail of the murders. Percy visibly shuddered as he described the final barbaric moments of Wesley Crandall's life: The punch that, just hearing it, made his stomach lurch. The surreal leap onto the man's prone head, as if it were a game of smashing watermelons. The taut strings of tension in his spine that left welts on his soul when two guns misfired. Then the explosion of the shotgun and the single blast that launched Crandall into eternity.

Percy continued to answer questions, retelling the events of the murderous mayhem that was Jerry Thompson. The jury sat frozen and took shallow breaths, as if they were watching a horror movie and could not look away. But this was no Hollywood entertainment. This was senseless slaughter and it was very real.

When questioning Percy about the Brookville Road murders, Sells deliberately slowed the questioning down. Had he or Thompson ever been there before? Had they met the victims, Melvin Hillis and Robert Beeler? No? Hillis and Beeler were just a couple of guys, finishing up their business day, looking forward to supper and an ordinary evening with their families.

But the details of the shootings, up close and personal, would normally indicate a crime of passion, a long-held hatred at the very least. Thompson had walked up to the men to blast them directly in the neck and face. Yet Percy insisted the killings were random. Thompson's only regret seemed to be that Percy did not find additional cash in the filing cabinet.

As Percy ground out the chilling details, the seconds ticked by like an agonized heartbeat. The families of the slaughtered men looked ill. Neither man had a chance. They had cried out to God while their bodies were shattered by bullets.

Thompson's expression of bored irritation never flickered.

Sells asked for all the details. Although he could state the facts in his sleep, the jury was hearing Percy's story for the first time. Sells wanted to be sure that the information they heard was complete and clear.

Percy said that he and Jerry Thompson did not frequent bars. Except for one trip to Houston, it was unusual for them to make trips together. On Valentine's Day, 1991, Percy joined Thompson on a jaunt. He went to New Castle that day simply because he was invited. Percy said, "He had met somebody in New Castle that his brother was selling some pot to, a couple ounces, I guess, for some money. He met him and he was going to go back there and see—he had just gotten some money from Shawn for insurance or something like that.

"He had a bunch of money. He just got $600 from somebody else a couple of days before that. He was going to make a deal and buy a quarter pound and bring it back to Indianapolis and sell it, but he was going to see if he could get a front and go back to New Castle and sell the stuff for that guy so he would make money doing that."

So, Thompson was buying and using pot while living in Percy's house? Percy took a defensive stance. "I don't know what he did when I was not there. I never seen him do it. He always had pot. He was always smoking it."

Percy insisted that until the idea of purchasing pot from Crandall was introduced, he did not know that Thompson was buying and selling marijuana.

Percy could not even testify as to where Thompson obtained his pot. He said, "Well, I don't know. I knew he had it. I don't know if he was buying it or not." Jerry could have gotten the pot from his brother David. "I never bought any pot from Jerry."

While living with the Percy family, Thompson and McCormick were neither paying rent nor helping with utilities. Percy said, "Every once in a while, he would go out and buy food. He was not really there to eat. Him and Shawn would go out to eat."

In regard to the February 14, 1991, trip to New Castle, Percy maintained that he had no foreknowledge that robbery and murder were the purpose of the trip. His understanding, based on what Thompson told him was as he had previously stated. "He wanted to go see this Wesley Crandall to buy a quarter pound of pot and possibly get another quarter pound and sell it for him. That's all."

CHAPTER 23—IN THE SHADOW OF THE GIANT

At the time of Crandall's murder, Percy worked 3:00 to 11:00 p.m. shifts at the Kroger central bakery. That week in February, he was on vacation. "My wife was working and the kids were in school and Shawn was asleep. It was cold outside and I did not have anything to do."

He did not worry about being caught with half a pound of pot. "I was with Jerry Thompson, and Jerry could handle anything."

The pair took along a 12 gauge shotgun that Jerry cut down in the garage and put back together in Percy's house. Later, investigators asked Percy if he knew that the shotgun was an illegal weapon once it was sawed off. "I didn't know that it was illegal as far as that you could not buy them and sell them. I didn't know anything about them," Percy said.

There was also the issue of Thompson dealing pot at Percy's house. Didn't he have a problem with that? Percy was noncommittal. "I really didn't think about it much."

Defense Attorney Jeffery A. Baldwin asked Percy point-blank, "Did you make any attempt to stop Jerry from shooting Wesley Crandall?"

"No."

The murder and the robbery had happened just as he said, Percy maintained. He had been in fear for his own life. He had neither said nor done anything that might arouse Thompson's ire at him. Thompson might have been chatting buddy-buddy with him, but he still had a loaded shotgun, and a lethal fist.

Once the pair returned to Percy's house, Jerry turned his attention to the stolen goods and "went through it all. He showed me and told me what it was," Percy stated. "There was a .22 Derringer, a nine-millimeter revolver, an M-10 and M-11, and a nine-millimeter pistol, semi-automatic." Also, "boxes of shells and a bag of loose shells." And "a knife that said 'Tiger' on it and a bag of pot."

For his participation in the crime, Percy was offered none of the pot. "I do not smoke pot," he said. "What would I want pot for?" Percy did admit that he had taken the occasional social puff or two that maintained his aura of friendship with Thompson.

The only thing Thompson gave him from the Crandall murder, Percy claimed was a knife that said "Tiger" on it. "I went to work and cut it up and got rid of it," Percy said.

Percy made his first attempt to report the murder on March 18, 1992. He explained the delay. "I didn't know what would happen. If my family was involved in it, they could die and I could die. I really didn't know what to do. I didn't, my head was kind of messed up."

Thompson's defense attorney looked incredulous. "Yet you continued to allow Jerry to live in your home? Even though you claim you were present during the time he murdered and robbed an individual?"

Percy struggled to describe his growing fear of Thompson. "By September of 1991, Jerry was going wild." After he moved from Percy's home, he was living with a woman named Janette, whose daughter was friends with Doug's daughter. "I went to the apartment to pick up my daughter and Jerry had guns laid out all over the place."

Percy helped Thompson get a job as a bartender at a tavern. "Then all these Outlaws were coming in. He got involved with the Outlaws motorcycle gang."

The violence kept erupting. "And then somebody touched or did something to [Thompson's brother] David's wife, where she works as a dancer and the guy just happened to walk into the same bar that he was bartending at. Dee was crying about it." Jerry and David Thompson shoved the man outside.

The beating that followed was brutal, Percy said. "David went out there and kicked him until his eye fell out." The man had blood running from his ears. He was beaten to a pulp.

Everyone ran but Percy remained behind. "I was the last one standing there until the police came up." He told the police nothing. "After somebody came to help the guy, I left."

Percy shuddered. "All this stuff was adding up and adding up." Then Percy got arrested for changing a vehicle identification number (VIN) on a vehicle. "I went to jail and got out. No big deal. I did not have anything to do with it anyway. That was the truck he [Thompson)] had before he moved into my house."

Percy's arrest changed nothing but, "Then after a little while longer Jerry got arrested. As soon as he got behind bars, I was able to go forward. The main reason was because he called me on the phone and said he is going to reach out and touch my family and take care of my family." And then, "His brother told me more or less the same thing."

After that, Percy contacted an attorney.

So, had he really reported the murder because he was worried about a VIN charge and a phone call from the jail? Thompson's defense attorneys challenged that Percy had concocted his story solely for the purpose of gaining immunity.

The VIN case was a Class C Felony, carrying a sentence of two to eight years, probably a suspended sentence with probation. But, if he had been charged as a participant in the Wesley Crandall murder, he could serve thirty to sixty years.

He could get life. Or death. Wasn't that motivation enough for him to go and tattle to the police?

Plus, Percy carried property from Crandall's residence. Had anyone told him that robbery with a deadly weapon carried a six- to twenty-year penalty? Did he understand the possible penalties he might face had he not been granted immunity in this case?

When confronted with a list of the multiple crimes he could have been convicted of—had he not been granted immunity by the State—Percy realized, "I could be in prison for the rest of my life or the death penalty, I guess." He admitted that part of his motivation to come clean was "to stay alive."

"But the thought of spending the rest of your life in prison did not have anything to do with it?" Thompson's attorney challenged.

"I did not think about it," Percy insisted. "I never thought about it before. Why would I think about it then? I did not go forward the first time or second time. He was still out."

But Thompson's attorneys were quick to point out that when Percy approached the State, he insisted upon immunity to avoid jail time.

"I did not insist on it. It was offered," Percy countered.

He had not spoken about the event at all before March, 1992. In October of 1991, Detective Tom Minor and another detective had come to his home to question him about Thompson in regard to a double homicide on La Salle. He admitted he was not honest with Detective Minor at that time.

"Because if I told him right then what I knew, then Jerry is going to find out and he will be over at my house." Thompson had lived with the Percy family from January to July of 1991. He moved out the first week of July, when he and Shawn broke up and he went to live with another girl.

Percy said that in April or May of that year, he told Thompson he wanted him to leave, but he could not remember the reason. It was possibly that, "He did not like my wife because she would not listen to him."

Confronted, Thompson refused to move out. Percy felt stuck, "because I was intimidated. I did not push it."

Then, "After the Wesley Crandall thing there was nothing I could say to him. There was not a thing I could say." Although there were other frictions, "I just tolerated him. I did what I had to do."

Once Thompson was behind bars, Percy started giving statements to law enforcement. He made his first voluntary statement to the Indianapolis Police Department on March 18, 1992. On May 12, 1992, he made a statement to Indiana State Police Detectives Butch Baker and Rick Shoemaker. He made a third statement on May 13, 1992, at the New Castle Police Department. His immunity meant that that he would not be charged with any crime he testified about, as long as he had not committed any murders or unless he lied, in which case he could be charged with perjury, and also with the other crimes.

After Percy approached the Marion County Prosecutor's Office with information about the murders, the VIN charges were dropped. Thompson's attorneys tried to claim that Percy's testimony had been bribed.

"Has anyone from the Marion County Prosecutor's Office ever threatened you with charging you with anything to do with the Brookville automotive murders?" they asked. "Was it your understanding that your cooperation resulted in those charges being dropped?"

Percy said no, but Thompson's attorneys continued to browbeat him.

At his initial meeting with law enforcement, Percy had met with detectives for many hours, discussing his information and giving a taped statement. There were two taped statements, one that ended at 6:04 p.m. and one that began at 6:19 p.m. Asked why, Percy replied, "All I know is, that it was a long day, that didn't end until 9:30 p.m. Maybe the detectives changed tapes."

Yes, a long day, the defense attorney pondered for the jury. Because Percy was questioned for a couple of hours before the tapes began. Didn't that sound suspicious?

Percy responded, "I had to tell them first. Then they wanted to put it in order and put it on tape, something like that." He added that, "they had different cases, I think Detective Phillips separated his and they continued with me being there... I went through the whole thing. I don't know if it was twice. I think it was separated into sections."

Percy described Thompson as six feet four, 320 pounds. His hair was mid length in February, 1991, at the time of Crandall's murder. "But in March he tried to cut it into a Mohawk. It came out messed up and he shaved it off."

When Thompson moved from Doug's house in July, 1991, he left behind some boxes of personal effects in the garage, as if he expected to come back. Percy claimed he never went through those boxes, but the police did. "My wife, Jerry's mother, and Shawn also went through the boxes. They just looked at pictures and wrapped up glass objects." After the police finished searching the boxes for evidence, Shawn McCormick picked them up.

Thompson continued to come by and visit Percy at least weekly with his new girlfriend, Janette. Were they still friends? Percy claimed that they were not. "I don't know how to put it in words. I do not have a degree to explain that relationship."

Was there anything in particular that made Percy dislike Thompson?

"Well, all of the things wrapped up together plus my youngest daughter complained about him." Thompson insisted it was a misunderstanding and Percy did nothing about it. He thought it was pointless to again ask Thompson to move out, and he was afraid to make a report to the police.

Thompson had already told Percy, "That I have no choice but to be his friend. I have no choice but to be with him. We are going to be together the rest of our lives according to him."

"He did not say he was going to beat you or shoot you or anything specific?" Baldwin probed.

"Well, a 200-pound axle thrown at you kind of makes you jump." The attack occurred when Percy first told Thompson he wanted him to move out. "I had to act like I was his friend," Percy insisted. Even when incarcerated, Thompson continued to call Percy from jail, making threats. After about twenty calls, Percy changed his number. He spoke to Thompson no more after that.

CHAPTER 24—A
DEFENSIVE ATTACK

Douglas Percy had told Sergeant David Phillips of the Indianapolis Police Department that he witnessed the shooting deaths of Robert Beeler and Melvin Hillis in the office of the car lot owned by Hillis at 5550 Brookville Road in Indianapolis. Phillips wrote, "Among the evidence recovered when the crime scene was processed were several 9mm shell casings and spent 9mm bullets."

From his March 18, 1992, interview of Percy, Sergeant Phillips learned that "after Hillis and Beeler had been shot, Thompson went through their pockets and removed cash, a wallet, and keys from the man who had been seated at the desk against the south wall of the office. Thompson then removed cash and a wallet from the man who had been seated at the desk against the west wall as he lay shot on the floor."

Thompson then fled the lot in a dark-blue 1978 El Dorado. That El Dorado, Thompson's most recent purchase, bore a paper plate in the driver's side rear window with dealer identification number 4908 M. Another witness identified the car.

Percy related what happened to the cash, wallets, and key rings. Those objects were evidence and Thompson wasted no time getting rid of them. Percy said, "Jerry took the cash from the wallets and the keys from the brown leather key ring. He then burned the wallets and their contents into ash with a cutting torch. He melted the keys by placing them on a concrete block and heating them with the torch."

So, proof of the robbery may have been eliminated, but Sells and Commons had the murder weapon lying in plain view of the jury. And they could document its journey to the courtroom. Witnesses and paperwork confirmed that the gun had belonged to Wesley Crandall. Thompson had been convicted of Crandall's murder.

The gun was used a month later to slay Hillis and Beeler and three months after that, it was seized from beneath Thompson's seat by Illinois State Police.

"Every step of the way," Sells stated, "this gun comes back to one person: Jerry Thompson. Is that right?" Percy said it was.

The testimony of Sergeant David Phillips added credence to the story, just in case there could be any doubt.

On June 6, 1991, Thompson and Percy were stopped in Illinois for a traffic violation. Illinois State Police Officer Kelly Hulsey seized two weapons. Percy said that the guns were a Mac-1 and the black semi-automatic pistol that Jerry Thompson had used to shoot both Robert Beeler and Melvin Hillis.

Having received this information, Sergeant Phillips moved quickly. It turned out that the guns were slated for destruction. Phillips reported, "On March 19, 1992, Detective Thomas Minor and I drove to Illinois State Police Post 12 in Heartland, Illinois. Upon our arrival there we met Sergeant Don Ziegler of the Illinois State Police. Sergeant Ziegler gave us a Stallard 9mm pistol, black in color and an SWD 9mm Mac-11 semi-automatic pistol. Sergeant Ziegler identified those pistols as the ones seized from Jerry Thompson and his associate by Trooper Kelly Hulsey on June 6, 1991, at or near Milepost 119 northbound on I-57 in Illinois."

The two Indianapolis officers took custody of the weapons and placed them in the Indianapolis Police Department property room the same day. The crime lab test-fired the weapons and confirmed that the rounds and casings retrieved from the double murder had been fired from the Stallard 9mm pistol obtained from Sergeant Ziegler.

Percy's story was backed up by more expert witnesses who verified the string of events that placed the gun in Thompson's hand on the day of the murders. The weapon had been sold to Wesley Crandall; there were records. Crandall's friends had seen the gun at his house before his murder. The guns taken by Thompson were not among Crandall's personal effects after he died. Thompson had been found guilty of Crandall's murder in a court of law.

Evidence tags showed that the guns taken from the van Percy and Thompson drove in June of 1991, had remained in Illinois State Police custody until the day Percy's statement led Indianapolis investigators to come looking for them.

Ballistics tests proved that only one gun in the world had fired the bullets that killed the two businessmen, and it was the same weapon that was found beneath Jerry Thompson's seat in the van in Illinois.

With all his evidence presented, Sells gave Thompson a huge smile. The Defense could get up and do a voodoo dance for all he cared; he knew Thompson was going down. Nothing would persuade the jury that he was an innocent man.

***

TV personality Mark Shaw, who appeared on a number of shows including ABC's *Good Morning America*, learned about the trial. Shaw's claim to fame was controversy. His books include *The Poison Patriot, Miscarriage of Justice: The Jonathan Pollard Story,* and *Melvin Belli: King of the Courtroom.* Shaw, who was an attorney and had been a former law associate of Larry Sells, wanted to testify on behalf of Thompson about the Wesley Crandall murder.

Thompson had already been convicted of that offense, and the facts of that case were only being used to show how Thompson obtained the weapon he used to kill Hillis and Beeler. As Shaw had no firsthand knowledge of either crime, Sells determined that his reason for being there was merely to push his own political agenda for potential use in a future book. He refused to let Shaw take the stand. The Defense did not allow him to testify either.

Shaw left in a huff. Later, he sent a fax to the Court, expressing his disappointment in Sells for prosecuting an innocent man. After all, two men had already pled guilty to the Crandall murder. Quoting seventeenth-century poet John Dryden, Shaw said, "Beware the fury of a patient man." It came across as a rather cryptic, ominous message.

Today, Sells notes that it has been over twenty years since that incident. "No fury yet. Damn patient, one would say."

Earlier near the end of the cross-examination of Douglas Percy, Jeffrey Baldwin made an uncharacteristic mistake. As he swarmed Percy, seeking to inject a bee sting of doubt into his story. Baldwin crossed his arms and swaggered toward Percy. "Oh, SURE this cock and bull story all happened, just like you said. Sure, it did. Then tell us, Mr. Percy, if you were so terrified of my client, or if you were ever such good friends, then why the sudden change? What prompted you, all of a sudden, to turn on him?"

"Because he molested my daughter!" Percy exploded. "She said he licked her privates one day." His words, echoing off the walls, had a ring of truth. Baldwin wisely stepped back. He did not want the jury to hear any more. All over the courtroom, angry eyes darted toward Thompson. Percy had already testified that his daughters were children, aged eight to thirteen when Thompson lived with them.

Sells examined the faces of the jurors. Percy's outburst appeared to affect the jury more powerfully than the details of Crandall's murder had. Thompson looked even more dangerous to them.

Changing to a softer tone, Baldwin eased into his next questions. He tried to imply that the alleged crime against his child drove Percy to frame his friend for murder.

The jury was not buying it. They knew they were looking at a convicted killer, a man who would leap up and try to crush another man's skull before blasting him with a shotgun. Surely such a soulless killer was capable of firing a gun into another man's face.

All of the evidence upon which the jury must rely in rendering a decision as to Thompson's guilt had been presented to them. There only remained the final arguments from the Defense and the Prosecution before the Court would read the final instructions on the applicable law, and the jury would retire to deliberate.

Defense Attorney Jeffrey Baldwin knew, as he stood to argue, that this was realistically his best opportunity to save Jerry Thompson's life. If he was convicted of the execution-style murders of Melvin Hillis and Robert Beeler, the jury would likely recommend the death sentence, especially in light of the conviction for the murder of Wesley Crandall.

Baldwin argued that the wrong man was on trial; that the only person directly linked to the killings was the prosecution's star witness, Douglas Percy. Percy had not come forward until a year after the slayings to tell his story. Baldwin challenged nearly every aspect of Percy's testimony, attempting to damage his credibility and question his motives.

Baldwin tried to throw sand in the jury's eyes. If Percy knew so much about the murder, he had to be there. Why wasn't he on trial? He was surely capable of shooting a gun; he wasn't paralyzed. And how convenient was it that he blamed three horrendous but profitable murders on his "friend?" Perhaps he just needed a scapegoat for his own crimes?

Anyone could have shot that gun, the Defense argued. Except for the casings, there was no evidence. If Thompson had shot the men at close range, where were his bloody clothes? Had investigators come forward with his shoe prints, fibers from his clothes, gunpowder residue on his hands? Of course not.

If Thompson had robbed a car dealership, where was the money? Thompson spent less than $200 the following week, and then he was too broke to make a weekly car payment. Did that sound like the rewards of a big robbery? Two hundred dollars could have come from anywhere, his job for instance.

And how did it happen that Percy seemingly "forgot" about these murders and continued to hang around with Thompson? Wasn't everything just fine and dandy between them until Percy figured out how to finger his buddy for his own crimes? Why would he turn on a good friend that he liked well enough to take into his home?

"Douglas Percy is a liar. He admitted to you from that witness stand that, 'No, I don't always tell the truth.'" Baldwin told jurors. "The State has spent a lot of time trying to prop him up."

He said the prosecutors tried to portray Percy as a "good Samaritan" who came forward to do his civic duty.

"No. He got an attorney and came forward and said, 'Let's make a deal.' And behind door number 1, we are going to let Douglas Percy get away on a C Felony and two to eight years in prison for a vehicle identification number charge to be dismissed and there would be no murder charges filed against him. Pretty sweet deal for a guy involved in the murders of three people," Baldwin charged.

"Douglas Percy is as shaky as the last leaf on a tree in late fall," Baldwin added. "Mr. Percy's been bought and paid for in a lot of ways, yet we are supposed to believe his story."

"He is going to be out living, doing his own thing even though he participated in three murders."

Baldwin argued that the standard of proof beyond a reasonable doubt had not been met and "the evidence presented to you is not even enough to conclude that Jerry Thompson was in Indianapolis that day, let alone convict him of murder."

CHAPTER 25—CRUSHING REASONABLE DOUBT

Time for the Prosecution to convince the jury that Jerry Thompson was guilty, guilty beyond any reasonable doubt. Wearing his Old Glory final argument tie, Larry Sells stood before twelve members of the community who were there to decide Thompson's fate. Sells knew Thompson was guilty and hoped these twelve men and women knew that too. He meant to make sure they did.

"On February 14th, 1991, Wesley Crandall Jr. was murdered in his home in New Castle. Sometime after that two retarded men were coerced into admitting that they killed Wesley Crandall; they were convicted and went to prison for crimes they did not commit, and but, for Doug Percy—" Sells turned to Percy and made sure the jury did the same. "—coming forward, they would probably still be there.

"He also solved the murders of Melvin Hillis and Robert Beeler that occurred at Hillis Auto Sales down on Brookville Road, just one month later, March 14th, 1991; the police were stymied and had made no arrest in that case."

The jury's eyes flickered again toward Doug Percy. The State's star witness, a Mighty Mouse hero, sat quietly as if embarrassed by the attention.

Sells continued. "If Doug Percy hadn't come forward when he had, part of the evidence in this case would have been lost; maybe the most important piece of physical evidence in this case would have been lost. You heard from Illinois State Trooper, Sergeant Don Ziegler, that they were getting ready to destroy this gun, State's Exhibit #1. Doug Percy told Indianapolis Police Detectives about this gun, and about the fact that the Illinois State Police had it. The gun had been taken from Jerry Thompson by Trooper Hulsey when Thompson and Percy were stopped on June the 6th, 1991."

Sells changed his stance and his tone. He did not intend for the jury to regard Percy as a hero. Sells kept a professional demeanor but the merest flush of anger bled through his face. This was no mere story. These were facts of life and death.

"Unfortunately, he came forward about thirteen months later than he should have," Sells reminded the jury. "He came forward and saved those two young men from New Castle who were wrongfully convicted. However, we all wish he had come forward, sooner, before March 14, 1991. If he had, Melvin Hillis and Robert Beeler would still be alive, spending their lives with friends and family. That's something Doug Percy is going to have to live with every day for the rest of his life.

"All of us know Doug Percy is not blameless, and at the very least, he assisted Jerry Thompson after these horrible murders were committed. And, I emphasize 'after'; the evidence shows that he did nothing to kill any of those three men. He did not break five-foot, ten-inch, 160-pound Wesley Crandall's neck. He didn't stomp on him; he didn't take a shotgun and nearly blow his head off."

Sells directed the jury's attention to the Brookville Road murder weapon, a black and brutal looking firearm. "He didn't take a gun, this gun, and walk up and execute Melvin Hillis, stick the gun under the desk and execute Robert Beeler—he did!"

Sells whirled around forcefully as if he were throwing a hardball at Thompson's face. Thompson, not expecting Sells's thunderclap, looked alarmed.

Then Sells leaned toward the jury, making sure they caught every word. "Douglas Percy watched Jerry Thompson do those horrific things; and he followed Thompson's orders, in each instance, on February 14th, 1991, and March 14th, 1991, and carried items both out of Crandall's house and out of the car lot," Sells reminded the jury. "Two of those items are State's Exhibit #1, and the M-11, State's Exhibit #51, the guns found by Illinois State Trooper Hulsey on June 6, 1991, when he stopped Doug Percy and Jerry Thompson in their vehicle on Interstate 57 in Illinois."

Now Sells dropped all emotion. His voice became steel, mirroring Thompson's inhuman lack of compassion. "Jerry Thompson, as you've been told, had a philosophy about the commission of these robberies and murders and how to avoid detection; you heard the testimony of Doug Percy. Jerry Thompson told him that, if you kill those people, there will be no witnesses; 'No witnesses, no problems.' He got Doug Percy, through whatever means, to help him, so that he would not have to worry about Doug Percy going to the authorities. And, being the only witness, that would be a problem."

Did this reality send a chill through the jury? It looked like it did. A number of them nudged forward, interested in what came next.

Sells said, "Don't misunderstand me; Doug Percy is a coward; his actions and inaction, led to the deaths of three people. But, without his help Jerry Thompson could still be out there robbing and killing people.

"You may ask yourselves; how can you be certain that Douglas Percy has told you the truth? From his vivid description of what occurred during those murders on February the 14th, and March the 14th; you can have absolutely no doubt that he was there, that either he did it or he saw someone do it."

Almost imperceptibly, some jurors began to nod. Sells continued, "He admitted to you that he carried that shotgun into Wesley Crandall's house; he didn't have to tell you that, or tell the authorities that. He could have said, you know, 'I just walked in there, Jerry Thompson had the shotgun. I just thought he was going in there to buy drugs, and took the gun to feel safe.'"

Sells took a beat to let that sink in and then slowed his words.

"And he told you about how Jerry Thompson had struck Wesley Crandall, and how Jerry Thompson said, 'His neck is broken.' And how Jerry Thompson twice tried to shoot Wesley Crandall, twice the guns wouldn't fire, but on the third time, put a pillow over Wesley Crandall's head and shot him right in the temple. You heard Dr. Hawley, the pathologist, confirm that in fact Wesley Crandall was killed by a shotgun blast to the head."

Jury heads nodded yes. Seeing this agreement, Sells picked up the pace of his narrative again and began to fire off his arguments.

"Do you have any doubt that Doug Percy was there? You heard Doug Percy tell you about the Hillis sales office, and watching Jerry Thompson gun down those two men.

"He told you about hearing five or six shots and seeing how Jerry Thompson walked in, shot Melvin Hillis, walked over, stuck a gun under the desk and shot Robert Beeler.

"Percy's description of those events is corroborated by other evidence. Dr. Hawley told you there was a six-and-a-half-inch stippling pattern on the face of Robert Beeler; Evan Thompson, the crime lab forensic firearms expert, testified that the six-and-a-half-inch stippling pattern meant the gun was fired from approximately a foot from Robert Beeler's face."

Sells splayed his hand in front of his own face. It was a small gesture, but the effect on the courtroom was chilling. He turned a brief, compassionate gaze on the families of the victims. They should not have to hear this, but reliving the pain, and hearing the hard evidence, was the price of justice.

He continued, "And Dr. Hawley said that in all probability Robert Beeler was shot while he was lying underneath that desk.

"How could Doug Percy have known those things had he not been there, and either did it or saw it done?

"So, again the question is who committed the murders of Melvin Hillis and Robert Beeler?

"The Defense has tried to suggest that someone other than Jerry Thompson was with Percy during the robbery and murder of Melvin Hillis and Robert Beeler. That maybe it was State's witness Michael Featheringill that witness Michael Lake saw on the car lot that day with Percy. Lake, while leaving Hillis Auto Sales, saw two men entering the lot in a large dark-blue automobile. He was too far from them to be able to make an identification of either man. He told you that one was significantly larger than the other. At six feet four and 300 pounds, Jerry Thompson certainly was significantly larger than the five-foot-ten slender Doug Percy even sitting in a car. And Lake, when shown a photograph of Thompson's big dark-blue Eldorado Cadillac, indicated that it sure looked like the car he saw that day. It was not Mike Featheringill's brown Cutlass Supreme."

Sells gave the jury an almost imperceptive shake of his head. In the solemn courtroom, a number of jurors mimicked him, unaware that they were shaking their heads "no." He did not turn his head, but he could sense the families of the murdered men also shaking their heads and sending silent, agonized pleas for the jury to see the truth that would un-muddy the waters and bring them clear closure.

"The Defense wanted to discredit Michael Featheringill because of the damaging testimony he provided against their client," Sells explained. "Remember, Featheringill testified that sometime around his birthday of February 14, 1991, Thompson showed him a shotgun, a 9mm semi-automatic handgun, and a 'pit bull' gun. Featheringill told you that State's Exhibit #1 looked like that 9mm Thompson showed him. You heard that a shotgun was used to kill Crandall on Featheringill's birthday February 14. And that a 'pit bull' gun and a 9mm semi-automatic were taken during the robbery and murder of Crandall. Columbus gun shop owner Velma Brown said she sold those guns to Crandall."

Sells mimed the sleight of hand that revealed a magician's trick. "What better way to discredit Featheringill than by creating the impression that he was one of the killers?"

Sells paced before the jury box now, drawing their attention to Percy and away from Thompson. His hands, palms up, suggested the need to reason together.

"What motive, Ladies and Gentlemen, would encourage Doug Percy to come forward if he was the person who killed those people? Would he come forward because he had been arrested for altering a vehicle identification number on a car, charged with a Class C Felony? Is that enough to make him come forward and implicate himself in three murders?

"And why would he pick this mountain of a man to blame for these murders? A man, who if he was so inclined, could snap Percy's neck like a Thanksgiving Day turkey wishbone. You heard about that 200-pound truck axle that Thompson hurled like a javelin at Percy. Hell, name anybody but him unless you feel compelled to tell the truth. If Percy decided to tell the authorities about his involvement, no reason to lie about who was with him.

"Even if Percy receives immunity, he's subjecting himself and all the members of his family to the indignity of knowing that Doug Percy had participated in those murders. He's risking losing the job that he held for years at the Kroger Bakery. If his employer were to find out about Percy's involvement in multiple murders, he would probably terminate him.

"A day after the robbery and murders of Melvin Hillis and Robert Beeler, Jerry Thompson walked into the car dealership where he had purchased his large dark-blue Eldorado Cadillac and paid employee George Sexton

$152.25 toward his $40 weekly payment and also paid the rest of the sales tax he owed from the purchase. Where did he get that money? He did not have a job. Not long after that, the car was repossessed because he had made no further payments."

Holding State's Exhibit #1, the 9mm Stallard in his hand in front of the jury, Sells said, "Remember the testimony of firearms expert Evan Thompson? His examination revealed that the spent bullets and fired shell casings found at the murder scene and the bullet removed from the body of Melvin Hillis were all fired from this gun, to the exclusion of all other guns in the world. That he was absolutely certain that his examination results would be confirmed by any other qualified firearms examiner. That is proof beyond any doubt. This IS the murder weapon."

Sells asked the jury to remember what Jeffrey Baldwin had just told them, that "The evidence presented to you is not even enough to conclude that Jerry Thompson was in Indianapolis let alone convict him of murder."

Sells thrust his hands toward the jurors. They held State's Exhibit #1 and the bullets and shell casings recovered from the scene and the bullet removed from the body of Melvin Hillis. "Really, Mr. Baldwin? Well, this 9mm Stallard was sure as hell in Indianapolis that day. And it fired the bullets that killed those innocent men Melvin Hillis and Robert Beeler. And where was this gun, Jerry Thompson's favorite gun, found less than three months later? It was found by Trooper Hulsey under the passenger seat in which Jerry Thompson was sitting when Hulsey stopped the van driven by Doug Percy on June 6, 1991.

"This gun, State's Exhibit #1, came out of Crandall's home, just as Doug Percy said. This gun was used to kill Melvin Hillis and Robert Beeler just as Doug Percy said, and Jerry Thompson had this gun when stopped by Illinois State Trooper Hulsey. That corroborates the testimony of Doug Percy."

Sells reminded the jury that court had not convened to discuss what might have happened, but to prove the truth of the actual events.

Percy had been sitting hunkered down, shame-faced, but he sat up now and dared a few cautious glances at Thompson. The Defense Attorneys appeared to be reminding Thompson to remain calm, but in that moment, Jerry Thompson's anger bled forth and he looked like the killer he was. He emitted a low growl in Percy's direction and his attorneys whispered to him sharply.

Sells sent a brief, sarcastic smile to the defense table and turned his attention back to the jury. He wanted them to hear more. "Doug Percy testified that he stopped at Hillis Auto Sales to look at a car he had seen there while driving to work at the nearby Kroger Bakery on an earlier date. It was a neat looking black Buick Riviera. After examining the exterior, he decided he would go into the office and get the keys to look at the interior and start the engine to see how it ran. He got the keys from either Melvin Hillis or Robert Beeler. Percy liked the car, but when he opened the hood, he noticed that some oil had leaked around the valve covers. He went back inside the office, joked with Hillis and Beeler and tried to get them to lower the price on the car. They laughed, said they would fix the leak, but the price would remain the same."

Sells stepped forward, arms out, expressing the camaraderie of the men on that chilly afternoon. Dusk was falling on Indiana, but inside that office there was warmth and friendship. Hillis and Beeler had been "the kind of men you could readily talk to for hours until Thompson entered and gunned them down," Sells told the courtroom.

"I guess someone with a creative enough mind could make all that up," Sells suggested, "and for what reason, I don't know, but it sounded, like it really happened, didn't it, that discussion took place and they were joking about it.

"Do you think he would be participating in that sort of conversation with them if he intended to gun them down? Why bother? Just walk in there and shoot them like Jerry Thompson did. You don't have to joke with them and carry on a conversation.

"Doug Percy, married, four children, worked at the same job for years; he took Thompson and his girlfriend into his home, thinking they were down on their luck; does that sound like a murderer? I mean he's not in a position where he's not working and sponging off other people; he's a productive member of society, trying to raise his family. Does that sound like a murderer?

"But, probably the most important corroboration is you hearing and seeing him testify from that witness stand; he wasn't some kind of blood-lusting brute, who brutalized and killed people; he was a coward, under the control of a demon."

Sells let that sink in.

"He didn't come forward until Jerry Thompson was not an immediate threat to him; and only then after he received several collect calls from Jerry Thompson, in which Jerry Thompson threatened, among other things, to 'reach out and touch' Doug Percy's family. He finally had the courage at that point to come forward; the evidence proves, Ladies and Gentlemen, that Jerry Thompson committed these unconscionable, horrific murders."

Sells believed the facts were enough to convince any jury of Thompson's guilt. He closed his argument, offering some imagery that he hoped would not leak easily from their minds.

"Behold the blue Cadillac, and 'His name that drove it was death and hell followed after him.'"

Sells raised his voice.

"Death to Melvin Hillis and Robert Beeler, and the final terrifying, agonizing moments before their deaths, they had no trial; their final plea, their last words, 'Oh, my God, no,' were answered with six bullets, four to disable them, and two to assure their deaths."

Sells followed this verbal punch with a quiet reminder.

"Jerry Thompson has had his trial, something he didn't give his defenseless victims; he's been fairly tried, and Ladies and Gentlemen, *he should be fairly convicted.*

"'Be sober, be vigilant, because your adversary, the Devil, is a roaring lion that walks about seeking whom he may devour.'

"I beseech you, convict this merchant of death, that he may not walk about and devour others."

CHAPTER 26—LIFE OR DEATH?

Awaiting the jury's decision, Sells and Commons ate several meals, food they were too tired to taste, and microscopically examined their case. Had they left anything out? Had the Defense team managed to present Thompson as a victim? Would anyone believe he was not a savage killer?

When the jury finally returned with a guilty verdict, it felt like the first sunlit day of spring. They had won. The families of the victims could have a modicum of peace. The two deputy prosecutors enjoyed a brief celebration with their families. Then they crawled back into their work cave. The sentencing hearing loomed, and they were going to battle for the death penalty. Thompson had destroyed so many lives—it was time for him to pay for those barbaric deaths.

The prosecution had nothing to add to their trial arguments. Thompson was a proven killer. Only his death would ensure that the public was safe from his murderous rage. He had made a career of being a prisoner; he wasn't going to improve with time.

In an effort to dissuade the Court against the death penalty, the Defense offered statistics from the Department of Corrections. According to their report, Indiana's current prison population numbered 16,172 prisoners. Of those, about 10 percent, 1,632 were serving time for murder convictions. Fifty-one of them resided on Death Row, a mere 3.1 percent, the Defense was quick to point out. Another seven had been sentenced to life without the possibility of parole. The remaining 96.8 percent—1,581 murderers, were housed among the general population of various prisons.

"The Indiana Department of Correction is experienced and well-able to incarcerate offenders convicted of murder and multiple murders in their general population," Thompson's attorneys declared.

The Defense also complained that Percy participated but was not being punished. "Can or should this Court sentence anyone to die on the strength of Douglas Percy's testimony?" they cried. "When faced with the decision of the ultimate penalty, Douglas Percy is simply not credible enough to warrant Jerry Thompson losing his life."

It was a terrible discrepancy, they pointed out. Thompson was already serving a ninety-year sentence while Percy continued to walk around a free man.

An *Indianapolis Star* article, dated March 13, 1996, read: "Jurors considering death for killer."

The death penalty phase of the trial continued Tuesday without Thompson after he decided he'd rather go back to the Marion County Jail than listen to the arguments before the jury.

One of Thompson's public defenders, Robert Clutter, said, "I think he was worried about the emotional strain. You can't really blame him.

Thompson also knew that no evidence to mitigate his involvement in the crimes would be offered to the jury, Clutter added. Defense Attorneys also feared Thompson's criminal record and suspected involvement in the La Salle Street murders would arise should he testify.

But Defense Attorney Jeffrey Baldwin told jurors that sentencing Thompson to death would serve no purpose.

Jurors were told Thompson could receive up to 161 years in prison but did not know he was also facing an additional thirty years for being a habitual offender.

***

Headache level tension pervaded the courtroom. All eyes were on the jury's indiscernible expressions as Judge Barney read them their instructions. They had found Jerry Thompson guilty of multiple murder. Now they must decide: Did his crimes justify the death penalty?

There was no way to predict how long the jury would take. For all the attorneys knew, there might be people on the panel who took half an hour to place a restaurant order. But Sells and Commons were veterans. They had tried murderers before. They let nothing shake their confidence. Thompson needed to leave this earth and settle his rage in a higher court.

When the jury filed back into the courtroom, people forgot to breathe. Judge Barney's face was expressionless. Thompson's attorneys were mannequins of decorum.

The jury that had convicted Jerry Thompson recommended that he be sentenced to death. Judge Barney agreed, and Thompson was shipped off to Death Row in Michigan City, Indiana.

***

Jerry Thompson met Jackie Bloomer through another prisoner's telephone conversations. On April 3, 1997, at age forty-one, Thompson married Jackie in the Death Row visiting room. Thompson's daughter Holly attended the wedding.

Jackie wore a black and white dress. She was four feet, eight inches tall, and fifty-nine years old. Thompson towered over his bride in his wedding garb of jeans and a blue work shirt. The marriage was never consummated. Their relationship consisted of letters and bimonthly visits. Jackie had been abused in other relationships. Jerry wrote to her, "You are a very beautiful woman, but you forgot that."

If everything had progressed as it should have, Thompson would have exhausted his appeals in ten to fifteen years and departed this earth by means of lethal injection, a much more humane execution than that visited upon his victims.

Those appeals, all that delayed Thompson's eternal appointment, were in the hands of a litany of Appellate Court reviewers. Sells saw little chance of any Appellate Court disturbing the jury's verdict.

But Sells was wrong. He did not take into account that the Indiana Supreme Court would overrule years of court precedent. They decided it was not fair to poor Jerry that the jury deciding his fate for a double homicide should be told that he had been convicted of another murder, one he committed just one month before he killed two Indianapolis businessmen.

The jury might have been biased, hearing how Thompson had nearly blown the head off a New Castle man with a 12 gauge shotgun. Never mind, the Supreme Court said, that he used one of the guns taken in that murder to commit the two murders for which he had received the death penalty.

The Court held it was okay to tell the jury he stole the gun, but withhold from them the information—in effect lie to them—about the murder being committed in the process. Sells did not agree with that ruling, nor did past Supreme Court decisions, but he was bound by it nonetheless.

Jerry Thompson would be remanded over for a new trial.

CHAPTER 27—TRIAL NUMBER TWO

In June of 2000, Jerry Thompson went on trial for his life for the second time.

For the second trial, Sells teamed up with Mark Massa, the Marion County Prosecutor's Chief Counsel. Massa is currently a Justice on the Indiana Supreme Court. To this day, Sells wishes Massa had been in that position on the Court when Thompson's appeal was considered. It would have saved the taxpayers the kingdom-sized bundle a new trial would cost.

At that time, Massa had never tried a death penalty case but had prosecuted nearly every other type of major felony. He had also served as a clerk for Randall Shepard, former Chief Justice of the Indiana Supreme Court. As Shepard's clerk, Massa wrote the legal opinions of several Supreme Court cases.

Sells and Massa were joined at the prosecution table by Kathy Cronley, Sells's trusted paralegal and ever-present trial sidekick. He claimed that it was largely due to her efforts that he never lost a homicide case.

The new Defense team consisted of Joseph Cleary, the attorney who had won the appeal, and David Hennessy, one of the best criminal defense lawyers in the state of Indiana. The law provided nothing but the best for the killer. Sells had observed Hennessy's sword-like skill in the courtroom, but he was not about to let the man slice up his case.

Sells always entered the courtroom believing he could win. He knew that some lawyers were more scholarly, better students of the law than he, but that did not mean they could beat him.

Sells had great respect for his legal adversaries, but he was not at all intimidated by them. He had bested Hennessy in a high-profile murder case a few years earlier. Plus, he had won fourteen homicide trials in 1997 following the first Thompson trial. Then in 1998, he won the most difficult and most satisfying murder conviction in his career against two nationally respected criminal defense attorneys. He had every reason to be confident. He also had Mark Massa, who possessed one of the finest legal minds in the State, as co-counsel.

A major concern going into the trial was that the Indiana Supreme Court had stripped the prosecution of its most significant evidence, that Thompson had killed Melvin Hillis and Robert Beeler with a gun obtained in a brutal robbery and murder just a month before.

Sells was convinced that if he could convict Thompson of the murders of Hillis and Beeler, he could also convince the jury to recommend the death sentence. If Thompson was convicted again of murdering the businessmen, the Prosecution could then tell them about the Crandall murder during the sentencing phase. Indiana law requires that before a jury can recommend the death sentence, the State must allege and prove certain statutory aggravating circumstances, in addition to the actual murder or murders for which a defendant is on trial. One aggravating circumstance alleged in this case was that Thompson had committed or been convicted of another murder. But the jury could not even be made aware of those allegations unless and until Thompson was found guilty of the underlying murders.

Cleary and Hennessy were dwarfed at the Defense table by Thompson, but they looked as vicious as he did. A pair of legal eagles, Thompson's team poised to pluck out Sells's and Massa's eyes. These highly seasoned attorneys dressed Thompson with scarves and turtlenecks, despite the June weather, to cover every one of the hate tattoos emblazoned on his skin. They had their client sit quietly at the table taking notes, as demure as a misunderstood Boy Scout.

The Criminal Court trial judge was Tanya Walton-Pratt, who was later appointed a Federal Judge of the United States District Court for the Southern District of Indiana.

Larry Sells meant for Jerry Thompson's escape from Michigan City, Indiana's Death Row to be very short lived. He was sending the Beast back to his hellhole and as far as he was concerned, the US Marines weren't going to stop him. This attitude served him well, because it appeared that the US Marines showed up to protect poor Jerry from legal harm.

The courtroom was packed with a veritable "Who's Who?" of anti-death penalty expert minds who were ready, willing, and able to lend whatever assistance Thompson's Defense Attorneys requested.

The Defense had that assistance, they had experience, they had the reputation, and they had the credentials. Sells swore they would never have his passion. He felt like he was standing in front of an oncoming freight train, but no train was going to stop him from sending the Beast back to Death Row. At the time of that second trial in 2000, Thompson had spent nearly all his adult years in prison. He certainly had not benefitted society when he was a free man.

Sells looked over the opposition. He was not fazed. Not even a little bit. He did not consider himself a legal scholar but Mark Massa was, and he was glad to have him as his co-counsel. At six feet, three inches tall and 200 pounds, Sells was not as big as Jerry Thompson. But he had kicked Thompson's ass four years earlier, and was certain he would do it again. He knew he could convince a jury to convict Jerry Thompson and recommend the death sentence regardless of who all represented him.

Before court began Thompson gave Sells a menacing stare, conveying to the prosecuting attorney that if there were not armed deputy sheriffs present, he would take Sells apart. Sells smirked. He was ready for war.

Douglas Percy's testimony was still solid. In pre-trial interviews, his story remained straight, shifting neither left nor right. Of course, he could not now testify in court to Wesley Crandall's murder; he also could not point to it as a source of the murder weapon.

Hennessy and Cleary had a talent for taking witnesses apart. Sells knew they would rip into Percy like a bear going after a honeycomb—if they got the chance.

Sells decided not to give them that chance. When he placed Percy on the witness stand, he asked very limited questions, mostly calling for yes and no responses. Had he seen the two murders? Did they happen on March 14, 1991? Did the murders happen at Hillis Auto Sales? Who had the murder weapon? Did he see Jerry Thompson shoot the two victims? Did the Illinois State Police take custody of that weapon three months later during a traffic stop?

Percy told the very basic facts of the murders to the jury. Yes, he was there. Yes, he saw Thompson shoot the two men. Yes, the Illinois State Police took custody of the murder weapon. When Sells concluded his direct examination of Percy, he thought, "Good luck cross-examining that." He had left only a sliver of material for the Defense to cross-examine Percy about.

Hennessy had clearly put together a chess game of moves to put Percy's testimony in check. He had expected Percy to repeat his lengthy story about his involvement with Thompson as he had in the first trial in 1996. Now all of Hennessy's playing pieces rolled off the board.

Surprised by Sells's short direct examination, Hennessy asked for a brief continuance, claiming he had exhausted hours preparing for a substantial cross-examination based upon Percy's testimony in the 1996 trial as set out in that trial's transcript. "We are not prepared to go forward at this time," he told the Court.

Sells had noticed early on in the trial proceedings that Hennessy had a very noticeable nervous tic. When agitated, Hennessy would rapidly jerk his head and neck to the right, sometimes repeatedly. It was amazing how many things Sells thought of to irritate Hennessy. By this stage of the trial, the tics were of such violence and frequency it appeared that Hennessy might break his neck. Although Sells did not wish him harm, he was enjoying the discomfort experienced by his adversary.

When he finally got around to questioning Percy, Hennessy had been thrown so far off his game that he made very little dent in Percy's credibility. He did manage, however, to upset Percy so much, that Percy blurted out that one reason he told on Thompson was because Thompson had molested his daughter, a déjà vu of the first trial. Should have seen that neck twitch then!

As in the first trial, Indianapolis-Marion County Crime Lab forensic firearm's expert Evan Thompson testified that the handgun that had been taken from Jerry Thompson by Illinois State Trooper Hulsey in the June 1991 traffic stop had fired the bullets that killed Melvin Hillis and Robert Beeler. Crime Lab criminalist specialist Michael Taylor identified crime scene photographs showing where fired shell casings, bullets, and other items were discovered inside the Hillis Auto Sales office. A crime scene video of the car lot and office was shown to the jury. Taylor pointed out where Hillis and Beeler were when they were shot.

Having given the Defense team virtually nothing to work with, Sells took his seat and waited confidently for the outcome. There were no witnesses who could say that Jerry Thompson did not murder Hillis and Beeler. There was no way to disprove that the gun found in Thompson's possession was the murder weapon. Witnesses who saw

Thompson's El Dorado at the murder scene could not testify that they had unseen it.

Hennessy's job was to convince the jury that the State had not proved Thompson's guilt beyond a reasonable doubt. He had done a good job of covering his client's tattoos and keeping him calm in the courtroom, but he had no evidence.

Looking offended, Hennessy approached the jury to give his final argument. It was downright rude for the Prosecution to stand up there and call Thompson a killer in front of God and everybody, he insisted. "How would you feel? How would your family feel if these horrid things were said about you with no evidence whatsoever?"

He pointed to Thompson as if he were a hapless victim. "They call this man a murderer, but where is the proof? Him?" He flung an accusing finger in Percy's direction. "He's just a storyteller, Ladies and Gentlemen. There is no proof, none whatsoever, that Mr. Douglas Percy is telling the truth." Was there anything, beyond his own self-serving words that made Percy a credible witness? "No. There is no reason for you to believe anything that man has told you."

Okay, maybe that particular gun was the murder weapon. But no one had stepped forward to prove that Percy had never touched it, that it was not in his own hands on March 14, 1991. "And when Officer Hulsey made his traffic stop and confiscated the guns, weren't there two men in that van? My client, Jerry Thompson, he was only along for the ride. He was only there because he had been invited—or more likely coerced—to help Douglas Percy hunt down a man who had stolen from him. Do you really believe that Mr. Percy went on that errand without a weapon? How else was he going to force that man to either come back to Indiana or cough up his money?"

Percy wasn't credible, Hennessy argued, because he was at the scene of a murder and like Pontius Pilate, he was washing the guilt off his own hands while blood ran down the faces of the innocent victims. He wasn't credible because, even if the murders went down the way he said they had, he had done nothing to help Hillis and Beeler.

"He says he stood there and watched a double murder like it was some action scene on a TV show and says he moved not one single muscle to help two men who were being slaughtered? Does that sound like a credible witness to you?"

And those other witnesses...who could really believe them? Somebody might have seen a couple of guys in a blue car. "How many blue cars did you pass on the way into this courtroom today? If there are two guys in a car, does that make either of them killers?"

Hennessy told the jury, "Somebody shot these men, but why should we believe it was Mr. Thompson? Do you really believe that Mr. Percy went to rob an auto dealership and didn't bother to take along a gun? Maybe he intended to talk them out of their money or beat them with his shoe? No. He might try to place his own guilt on Mr. Thompson, but he went into that dealership with a gun and he intended to use it."

Then there were the police officers "who supposedly investigated this crime. How far did that investigation go? Let's listen to the first guy who will speak to us. Let's just say that the first story we hear that sounds halfway plausible, that will be the best and the fastest way to solve this crime. Take a one-hour statement form Mr. I-know-all-about-it and *tah dah*! Crime solved."

Hennessy continued to question the validity of the State's witnesses, but he could not prove that any of them were lying.

"There is substantial doubt about Mr. Thompson's guilt in this matter and he should be found not guilty. How could anyone be convicted of murder based solely upon the testimony of Doug Percy?"

Judge Tanya Walton-Pratt called a brief recess at that point to allow the jurors and others to stretch their limbs and relax before final arguments resumed. Sells and Hennessy happened to meet up in the men's room. In the courtroom, the two men were combatants. In the neutral territory of the restroom, they were two men doing their best to serve justice, and they had respect for one another. Sells congratulated Hennessy, "Great argument, Dave!" Hennessy thanked him.

As Hennessy left, Sells said to himself, "But watch this: I'm going to resurrect two men from the dead!"

CHAPTER 28—A MATTER OF PERCEPTION

Larry Sells became a lawyer for fame and fortune. He had accomplished neither. But as he stood in the courtroom to convince twelve jurors to convict a psychopathic killer, there was no place he would rather be. There was a time when he had wanted to be a major league baseball player. He even thought that was a realistic possibility. But a shoulder injury helped convince him that there was a time to stop thinking about what he wanted to do and instead discover what he was meant to do.

Sells had also considered becoming an actor. He modeled, made a few commercials, even took acting lessons. Today he stood center stage in a real life-or-death drama in which those acting and modeling skills would be invaluable. He was meant to do this!

Sells did feel handicapped by the Indiana Supreme Court decision in this case, which stripped the prosecution of vital relevant evidence. He could not tell the jury that Jerry Thompson had obtained the gun used to rob and murder Melvin Hillis and Robert Beeler during the robbery and brutal murder of Wesley Crandall just one month earlier. There was nothing Sells could do about that. He must convince the jury based upon the evidence they had been permitted to hear.

David Hennessy had done his best to discredit the testimony of State's witnesses Mike Featheringill and

Michael Lake about their observations. He had viciously assailed the motives and credibility of Doug Percy. Sells had some damage repair to do.

"Mr. Hennessy has attacked me and most of the witnesses that Mr. Massa and I have presented to you," Sells told the jury. "I admit there are some minor conflicts in the testimony of certain witnesses. Whether Thompson's car was dark blue or brown. Whether his hair was shoulder or collar length. Are those really important matters? That is for you to decide. There are always going to be differences in the testimony of witnesses. I implore you not to decide this case over insignificant details. Base your decision on that evidence which most convinces you of its truthfulness in determining the guilt of the defendant.

"Remember, I told you during jury selection that this is not a perfect world and that there is no such thing as a perfect case. Never has been. Never will be. The State can not, nor is it required to, prove a perfect case. That is not to say that if you are not convinced beyond a reasonable doubt that the evidence proves his guilt, that he should be convicted. If you do not believe that he is guilty, send him home!"

Mr. Hennessy objected, approached the bench and quietly argued that "Send him home" was improper and the statement should be ordered stricken from the record. "Not at all," Sells countered. "Prison is his home." Hennessy still managed to get the comment stricken from the record. Sells may have lost the ruling, but he knew the jurors would not be able to purge from their minds the thought of their sending the Beast home. Because of the Supreme Court ruling, they had not been told that Thompson was already serving ninety years for an earlier murder. And for that matter, jurors did not even know that Thompson was confined.

"Let me give you an example of how people perceive events differently," Sells continued. "Even holy men describing the most significant events in the history of Christianity, the Crucifixion and Resurrection of Jesus

Christ, differed in their accounts. Matthew, Mark, Luke, and John, disciples of Christ, wrote in the Bible about what had occurred during those events. Their descriptions had differences but not as to the important matters. I will not detail those differences. There are those among you who are much more knowledgeable of the Scriptures than I. How can we expect ordinary folks like Michael Lake and Mike Featheringill to remember everything the same way when not even holy men can?"

He nudged the jury back to the life-and-death issue before them.

"Two good men are gone, gone forever, gone before their time, cut down by the murderous acts of a cold-blooded killer." Sells quoted eighteenth-century Scottish poet Robert Burns, "Man's inhumanity to man makes countless thousands mourn," and said, "The cruel inhuman acts perpetrated upon Melvin Hillis and Robert Beeler by Jerry Thompson, not only ended their lives but affected the lives of many other people."

He cited the testimony of seventy-one-year-old James Walton who worked at Hillis Auto Sales for thirty-six years. "Now that gives you some idea of the affection this man had for Mr. Hillis. It seemed that when he was telling us about his work there that he felt like he worked with Melvin Hillis and not just for Melvin Hillis, that they were a family there."

James Rayhill, the nephew of Melvin Hillis, and employees William Smith, Ralph Bradshaw, and James Walton continued to run Hillis Auto for a short time after the murders. But for all the Hillis and Beeler family and friends, "Jerry Thompson not only took their lives and destroyed their dreams and plans and ambitions he also destroyed the dreams and plans of many other people. He's on trial here for killing them and that's all I can ask you to consider, the robberies and the killings of March 14th, 1991."

Douglas Percy, Sells told the jury, was there to look at and possibly purchase a black Riviera. "But he didn't want to pay the asking price. After looking the car over, he went into the office. Mr. Hillis was seated at his desk on the far side of the small office. Mr. Beeler was seated just to the left as you entered. Percy's conversation with Hillis and Beeler was a friendly one. Percy was haggling over the price of the car because of a leaky valve cover gasket. The men shared a laugh about that. Hillis said that's no big deal. We can cover a gasket; it's certainly not going to drive down the price of the car that much."

Having set the scene, Sells asked, "Then does Percy just pull a gun and mow them down? Does he kill them after having that friendly little discussion? Why bother even talking to them in the first place? Just pull the gun and blast away. No reason for any small talk. Or did Percy just make up that little story? If so, why? Percy did not even have to admit he was in the office. Percy's testimony about the conversation in the office definitely has the ring of truth. And it also shows he did not know Thompson intended to come in the office and kill the men. Well, you be the judge of that.

"Without any doubt, we know that Melvin Hillis and Robert Beeler were killed inside the Hillis Auto sales office. The only eyewitness account is that of Doug Percy.

"I wish we could have two more witnesses testify for you in this case, two other people that were there when it happened, but I can't, they're gone. Wait a minute." Sells looked toward the heavens. "Melvin Hillis, would you come down here and tell us what happened? These folks want to know."

Sells gestured and altered his voice. "Well, I was sitting there at my desk…"

Hennessy, twitching like a cornered rabbit, tried to object but was overruled. The Court said, "He can make a demonstration."

Approaching the bench, Hennessy said, "This goes beyond a demonstration, he's pretending to be someone that was not a witness, certainly they're deceased and—"

"I don't think I'm going to fool these folks," Sells countered. "I'm only going to talk about the evidence."

"Okay, I'll overrule," said Judge Walton-Pratt. "Let's see what he does."

Calling upon his early training as an actor, Sells played out the scene for the courtroom. "I'm sitting here at my desk and Bobby Beeler and I are sort of chuckling over that young fella coming in, wanting to drive the price down on that black Riviera. And I'm finishing up my paperwork, I've already got the daily receipts written down on the Hillis Auto Sales paper, of the cash and the checks that were taken in. And all of a sudden this great big Goliath of a man fills the doorway to the office and he's got this big old black gun in his hand pointed at me."

Sells paused for effect, and then continued his role.

"I said something, I don't know what it was, next thing I know that gun's belching fire and bullets. I get hit a couple of times in the belly and chest and I fall—out of my chair against the wall. I hear another shot being fired and it sounds like Bobby Beeler's trying to dive underneath his desk, I'm sort of fading in and out. I'm up against the wall, this big man takes another step or two towards me, I see the gun, I turn my head, the bullet goes in my neck. I feel it and then everything goes dark."

"His spinal cord's been severed. He's dead," Sells said.

He continued the story from Robert Beeler's perspective. "Well I'm sitting here at my desk and we're kind of having a chuckle about that fella, about the price of the car and the leaky valve cover gasket and I just turned back around to my desk to do some work and I hear Mel Hillis yell, 'Oh, no.' I hear two shots, I turn around, I'm shot myself. I see this huge person standing there before me.

"The only thing I can think to do is drop, get beneath that table. I do it. I hear another shot but I don't look back and all of a sudden there's a shadow over me and next thing I know I get mule-kicked in the jaw and then the lights go out."

A moment of silence followed and then Sells said, "He's dead. Now Doug Percy told you what he saw Jerry Thompson do, he told you about the close proximity in which the gun was fired that shot Melvin Hillis. You saw where the bullet holes went through Melvin Hillis's neck and the bullet lodged in the wall right behind where he was sitting."

They had also heard how Thompson leaned down to shoot Beeler beneath the desk. "And you don't have to accept Doug Percy's word for that," Sells explained. "Look at where the evidence was found in this office. The shot, this last shot to Robert Beeler in the chin—wasn't it Evan Thompson who told you that this gun, State's Exhibit #1, ejects the cartridges out and back?

"There's the spent casing from that shot in this photograph, just as Doug Percy described to you, what he saw. Well, Doug Percy could have shot them. That's what Mr. Hennessy's trying to make you believe. Actually, either Percy or Thompson could have shot them. You have to decide which one did this horrible thing. That is your decision. But you do know that Percy was there when it happened as he said he was. How else would he have known about the details of the shootings?"

Sells asked the jury, "Doug Percy has lived at the same house on Routiers for thirteen years, married to the same woman, has four daughters, worked at Kroger for seventeen years and has another job that he's worked at for the last year and a half. He is working hard, earning money to support his family. Does that sound like the type of person that all of a sudden for no reason at all just goes in a car lot and guns down two innocent people?"

Thompson, on the other hand, had no money, Sells told everyone.

Hennessy objected, reminding the court that Thompson had worked at his brother's machine shop. The judge responded, "I'll overrule. The jury heard the evidence."

"Well I need to be entirely fair," Sells acknowledged, "He worked somewhere, but evidently it wasn't very consistent work because he couldn't even afford to have his own place. Doug Percy had to loan him money. Also, out of the goodness of his heart he had taken Thompson and his girlfriend, Shawn McCormick, into his home." Sells said, "You have a right to consider that evidence, along with all the other evidence you have heard in judging the credibility of Doug Percy."

There was a list of things that gave Percy credibility. "First of all, Doug Percy came forward. You can believe, if you want to, that he was scared to death of what was going to happen to him on these charges of altering the vehicle identification number on a car. You know, even if he was convicted, he could have either gotten a light sentence or probation. Do you think that's what drove him to talk to the police?"

In that situation, Sells explained, it would be expected that he would go to a lawyer first to represent him. "We are all entitled to legal representation especially when dealing with matters he was about to share with law enforcement." After Percy's attorney summarized what his client knew, an agreement was reached with the prosecutor's office that the VIN charge would be dropped in exchange for Percy's cooperation. The Prosecution agreed, as well, to extend immunity to Percy in exchange for his cooperation and truthful testimony against Jerry Thompson.

"But if we find out you're lying, no immunity." The criteria were explicit, Sells said. "If you were involved in the murder and robbery of Robert Beeler and Melvin Hillis then this immunity doesn't protect you from being charged for those offenses. Whoa!

"Now there's something different here, I'm not stumbling on a couple of little car cases. I, Douglas Percy, could be charged with murder if I don't tell them the truth and they find out I didn't? Phew... I myself could be facing the death penalty, they could send me up to Michigan City—this is back in 1991—and hook me up to Old Sparky and pull the switch."

Sells let that idea sink in and then said, "And he talked to the police and prosecutor anyway, and he told them what happened on March 14th,1991, knowing what could happen if it was discovered he lied.

"He could have just simply kept quiet. The authorities didn't know that he was involved or that he knew anything before he went to them. Just keep quiet, don't involve yourself in something like that. Why even take the chance?

"But he didn't. You know after witnessing something as horrible as what he saw, it would have to eat away at a person. It would fester like a big boil." Eventually, Percy had to lance that boil, get the poison out of his system and cleanse his soul, Sells told the jury. "When he felt less fearful of Thompson and more secure about his safety and that of his family, he came forward."

There were more reasons that Percy's testimony could be trusted. Percy said that Beeler was shot beneath the desk at close range. Crime scene photographs, physical evidence, and testimony from the pathologist Dr. Hawley and firearms expert Evan Thompson corroborated that. Percy said that Jerry Thompson went through the victims' pockets. Sells said, "You know that their pockets were pulled out, you saw that on the videotape. You know that whatever they had in their pockets was gone."

Then Percy had described how Thompson threw the men's wallets and keys into the middle of the floor and told

Percy to pick them up. He did. "Why did Doug Percy have to say that?" Sells questioned.

"Why, that makes him look like he took an active role in what happened, doesn't it? It makes him look like he's part of a robbery and murder by him picking up a wallet and keys and leaving with them. So, when you talk to the police, in order for it to look like you actually didn't do anything, leave that out, you don't have to tell the police that because they don't know that. The fact that he told them, in spite of how it made him look, shows you folks he's telling the truth.

"And how about him saying that Jerry Thompson told him to look in the file cabinet, see if there's any money in there? He didn't have to tell the police that, but he did.

"He has been questioned and challenged about these events at least six times. You have not heard any evidence that he has been inconsistent." Percy had not, as Hennessy claimed, created a story that made him appear innocent.

"He didn't have to admit that he asked Jerry Thompson to go to Texas. That makes it seem as if they are partners. He saw Thompson commit calculated, cold-blooded murders of two innocent, defenseless men. In spite of that, he still spent time with him and even asked him to go to Texas. He didn't have to tell anybody that. Percy is not stupid. He knows that makes him look bad, that he's still associating with Thompson after he's seen him do these things. But that makes his testimony more truthful, doesn't it, the fact that he's willing to admit that?

"You know he didn't have to admit on January the 4th, 1996, in his deposition that he lied to Detective Minor, lied to Detective Scruggs about something he was questioned about in October of '91 and January of '92, before he ever came forward. How does anybody but him know that he lied? But he admitted, 'Yeah, I lied to them. It was to protect Jerry Thompson. I lied to Detective Scruggs and I was protecting Jerry Thompson and me.'"

Referring to the movie, *Sergeant York*, the tale of a Tennessee mountain man who became "the most decorated hero in World War I," Sells described how Alvin York, played by Gary Cooper, was on his way to kill a man who had swindled him out of a piece of bottom land when he was struck by lightning. After this near-death experience, Alvin York did not want to kill anyone. He told his preacher, "The Lord sure does work in mysterious ways. I've seen the light. I'm a man of the Lord now."

Perhaps Percy also had a lightning bolt experience, Sells suggested. "I don't know what the source of that lightning was. Maybe it's just a coincidence that it struck him right before this gun, State's Exhibit #1, was destroyed, this gun that killed Melvin Hillis and Robert Beeler. Or maybe 'the Lord was working in mysterious ways.' This gun that is irrefutable evidence connecting Jerry Thompson to those murders was scheduled for destruction, but Percy gave his statement to law enforcement and the gun was recovered before that very important piece of evidence was lost forever."

Sells reminded the courtroom of the testimony of firearms expert Evan Thompson, who said he was one hundred percent certain that the bullets removed from the bodies of Melvin Hillis and Robert Beeler and the spent bullets and fired shell casings found at the scene were fired from this gun, State's Exhibit #1, to the exclusion of all other firearms in the world. "If Evan Thompson is one hundred percent sure, that is definitely proof beyond a reasonable doubt. This big guy used this big weapon to kill two innocent men on March 14th, 1991. The evidence is overwhelming that he did it.

"I asked you to consider all the evidence and carefully decide what this Defendant deserves for his conduct. It has been proved to you beyond a reasonable doubt. Decide this case without regard to what is facing you next. Heed the final words of Melvin Hillis before succumbing to the influence of Mr. Hennessy's arguments and acquitting his client and tell them, 'Oh, no. Oh, no.' You are guilty and we are going to convict you."

*　*　*

He was still guilty, and the jury said so.

Thompson grimaced like the Big Bad Wolf. Sells watched the killer huff and puff his way out the door under armed guard. Then he hefted his stack of files from the table.

Sells would get little sleep and too many quick sandwiches while he prepared for the penalty phase. He was rounding third base and no Defense team would block his charge to home plate. Thompson deserved the death penalty; Sells would accept no other outcome.

CHAPTER 29—THE BEAST ROARS

Not all murder convictions qualify for the death sentence: Only those prescribed by statute, such as the murder of a law enforcement officer (by definition a law enforcement officer includes a prosecuting attorney or a judge). Also qualifying are murders committed during robbery, rape, or certain other enumerated felonies. Conviction for an additional murder qualifies, as well. There are others listed in the statutes.

Death penalty qualifying offenses are called Aggravating Circumstances, and must be proved beyond a reasonable doubt just as the facts leading to the current murder conviction have been.

The State alleged that Jerry Thompson had intentionally killed Melvin Hillis and Robert Beeler while committing a robbery. It was also alleged that he had committed multiple murders and had been convicted of another murder, that of Wesley Crandall.

Since the jury had already convicted Thompson of the car lot robbery and murders, there only remained the task of proving that he had been convicted of the murder of Wesley Crandall. To do that, the State presented certified copies of the Sentencing Abstract on that case signed by the Judge of the Henry Circuit Court in New Castle, Indiana, and the Court's Judgment of Conviction of Jerry Thompson for that murder.

The Prosecution once again called Doug Percy to testify about the circumstances of the Crandall murder and to identify Thompson as the killer. Percy described the execution in graphic detail.

Thompson knocked the smaller man to the floor and jumped on his head and neck, exclaiming, "I think I broke his neck." Then he put a pillow over Crandall's head, presumably to prevent a blowback of blood and brain matter, and blasted the 12 gauge shotgun into the pillow at point-blank range.

Percy saw blood and human tissue oozing from beneath the pillow. By law the State could not present evidence about Thompson's other crimes spanning nearly two decades unless his attorneys screwed up and somehow "opened the door" for such additional evidence. Sells did not expect Hennessy and Cleary to make that mistake.

Sells could not tell the jurors about a call he had received, advising him that in his youth Thompson had killed an elderly woman in New Castle. Nor could he tell them about the murders of Allen White and Kathy Boggs in September 1991. Nor could Sells bring up Thompson's numerous convictions, including seven felony convictions including Child Molesting, Burglary, Escape, and others. Or that he had spent nearly all his adult life in prison. Or that while in prison he continued to break the law, sometimes committing violent acts against other inmates.

Thompson's life was a mess, all right, and it was about to get worse. During the penalty phase, the jury was allowed to hear that Thompson was already a convicted killer. They were informed that the "gentle giant" seated quietly at the Defense table, taking notes, had blasted a man's head with a shotgun.

Thompson did not respond to this information at all. His attorneys had done a great job of reining him in. They made a valiant effort to explain away Thompson's "mistake" "as a very bad day for him" "in the heat of passion" when he "could not control the anger broiling in his breast." Yes, it was too bad for Mr. Crandall, but he was, after all, a drug dealer, and that can be a dangerous business....

The Thompson siblings described the joys of their baby brother for the jury. Yes, he had gone wrong. He was a little messed up. Who wouldn't be, after being beaten and starved by their father? No one ever meant for little Jerry to turn out like this. He wanted to be in the military. He wanted to serve his country. He was a good person who wanted to help others.

He was helping other people now. Defense witnesses described how Thompson was using his time in prison, helping misguided youth through programs like Scared Straight. He was sending letters of fatherly advice to his daughter Holly and being an overall good guy, even behind bars. What would it benefit society if he were put to death? What could he continue to contribute, now that he was doing so much to help others?

Sara Thompson, Jerry's aged and ailing mother, suffered from rheumatoid arthritis and leukemia. Her visibly pained steps into the courtroom were a clear indication to the jury that her life had been difficult.

Sara had survived a brutal life and severe poverty. In an effort to care for her children she had deprived herself of clothing and basic necessities.

The depression had caused her weight to balloon up over 400 pounds, but she was getting it under control now. She, too, had been beaten by her husband and she could swear that he showed no mercy.

And now her youngest son was on trial for murder. And not just murder, but a senseless double slaying that netted him a few hundred dollars. Her testimony was that he couldn't have possibly done it. She didn't see how the jury found him guilty. And now they might sentence him to death? It was unthinkable. Surely the American justice system could see the value in her son's life. He was still young and had the potential to accomplish great things.

The Defense passed the witness, certain that Sara's heartfelt declarations had swayed the jury against the death penalty.

Sells approached the woman politely. "How are you today, ma'am? So sorry to put you through this, but the questions must be asked. You have told us about your son, Jerry."

"My baby. He's a good boy. If you just knew."

"He's the youngest? Of how many? How many children do you have, ma'am?"

"Five."

"Not easy to raise five children."

"No, sir."

"You were essentially a single parent? Carrying the load?" She nodded. "They all suffered from hunger, poverty, their father's rage?"

"They did. They did. God help me, they did. They all did."

The stress of her life had wrung Sara Thompson like a dishrag. This trial, this verdict, could only add to her grief. But this son of a safecracker and hog thief would wreak injury on his fellow man for the rest of his days. The jury could not see the human bomb before them.

Thompson's attorneys had wisely continued to dress him, despite the heat, in a high collar, long sleeves, and even a scarf to conceal the ocean of hate ink his body was submerged in. They had him sitting placidly at the defense table, pencil in hand, dutifully writing like a schoolboy. He did not look threatening at all. Just one more poor soul who'd made a mistake. A misguided individual who happened to be occupying the courtroom over the past days. Surely the jury would realize that and be kind.

That could not happen. Thompson was a man who was dangerous to others—all others. He needed to be executed to protect mankind, because he would always find a victim.

The jury needed to see Thompson's explosive nature. They needed to know that he was capable of immense destruction.

Sells gave Sara Thompson his full attention. "Five children," he affirmed, and then he pointed a finger at Jerry Thompson and shouted, "And how many of them turned out to be KILLERS?"

Thompson exploded out of his chair and roared! His placid features erupted into bestial angles. Both judge and jury lurched backward, almost breaking the backs of their chairs. "Stop this! Stop this right now!" he thundered. "I'm not gonna have my mom up there beggin' for my life for something I didn't even do!"

Despite the armed deputies in the courtroom, people cringed as if they were looking down the maw of a T-Rex. And they were.

Sells already knew that if Thompson could reach him, his life expectancy was about three seconds. But it had been worth the risk. Now the jury could feel the terror that had chewed into Hillis and Beeler when they were attacked suddenly and without warning.

The greatest impact was on Mark Massa. He was closest to the volcano when it erupted.

Once the deputies had forced Thompson back into his chair, the entire room took a collective, cautious breath. Sells turned his attention back to Sara Thompson. "I'm very sorry, ma'am," he said sincerely. "No further questions."

But the matter wasn't ended. Everyone in the courtroom had been singed by the lightning of Thompson's anger. For the safety of all present, Judge Walton-Pratt ordered that Thompson be manacled for the remainder of the proceedings.

Defense Attorneys Hennessy and Cleary argued that this was biased. The jury was not to see any prisoner shackled or in jail garb. It might make him look guilty! It was a violation of his rights!

But the Judge would not change her mind. Thompson would be restrained but they could put a skirt around the table so the jury could not see his chains. The Defense said this was also biased, so an identical skirt was hung around the prosecutors' table. Now there was no bias because no one could see Thompson's chains.

For the remainder of the trial, Sells took delight in stepping near Thompson, giving him knowing looks or smirking. Thompson responded with ferocious faces meant to intimidate his accuser. He also shook with rage and rattled his chains. No, the jury could not see them, but they were continually reminded that Thompson was chained, and they would never forget why.

Thompson's rage at Sells grew more palpable but Sells refused to be intimidated. In a few short hours, Thomson would return to sweat in his cell while Sells enjoyed a cold sandwich in the City Market. As the penalty phase wound down, Thompson caught the Judge involved in another matter and turned his soulless eyes on Sells. He was breathing fire at the deputy prosecutor.

Sells gestured back with an uplifted, open hand. Then he slowly curled his fingers until his fist was a rock. The meaning was clear to Thompson: *I've got you by the balls and I'm going to crush you.*

Prison was never going to help or change Jerry Thompson. He had now been an adult for twenty years and had spent seventeen of them behind bars. He wreaked havoc every time he got out. Rehabilitation? He'd had his chance.

The Defense called another mitigation witness to explain Thompson's psyche and aberrant behavior. Dr. Michael Gelbort, a neuropsychologist, testified that Thompson had a defect in the frontal lobe of his brain which limited his thought processes and caused him to be a follower and not a leader.

The Defense was still trying to create the impression that Percy had masterminded everything. The good doctor also testified that Thompson could be managed in a controlled environment. Clearly, that was support for the Defense team's position that Thompson need not be executed, merely confined in a secure setting.

Sells let Dr. Gelbort testify without objection even though some of the testimony was objectionable. On cross-examination, Sells only had one question. "Dr. Gelbort, can you assure us that Jerry Thompson will never kill again?"

The well-paid defense expert glanced at Hennessy and Cleary as if pleading for help, grimaced, then reluctantly said, "No, I cannot."

Sells looked at the jurors, then said "Thank you doctor. No further questions."

Sells then stared at Hennessy and Cleary, silently challenging them to call another witness. They did not.

CHAPTER 30—THE VALUE OF A KILLER'S LIFE

Only major league lawyers are offered the opportunity to present final arguments in a death penalty case. It is literally a "no holds barred" fight to the death between attorneys. David Hennessy was well prepared to present his final argument against Thompson receiving the death penalty. A veteran of the courtroom, Hennessy's strength was creating imagery with words, drawing the listener in. His talent would not be wasted on the jury. Knowing that Thompson's death would leave two daughters bereaved, his decision to compare his client to a small girl came across brilliantly.

"A long time ago a little girl named Annie was born. It was in an ugly environment and at the age of two, disease took her eyesight and she was blind and she became bitter and angry. And at the age of five they stuck her in an asylum in Tewksbury and her bitterness and anger turned into rages, which became violent and reclusive and they decided that she was hopeless and that nothing could be done with her and they stuck her in the basement of the asylum at Tewksbury.

"And there she would hide under a stairway and lash out at anyone who came near. As time went on an older nurse came to Tewksbury and she began taking her lunch on that stairwell, and she'd have her lunch and she'd read a book on the stairwell that little Annie was hiding under. Little Annie could hear the pages turning and she became curious and more and more curious and slowly she came out.

"And the older nurse reached out to her and slowly she responded until she would sit in the older nurse's lap and turn the pages as the nurse read to her. The nurse reached out to her, touched her, changed her, gave her hope.

"Then the director of the Massachusetts Board of Charities, Frank Sandborn, came to that asylum, he went down to the basement for some reason, he never had, no director ever had, this was the realm of the most unmanageable, the most hopeless, the abandoned, but he went down there and Annie heard him and Annie spoke and she said, 'Can I go to school?'

"He looked at her in disbelief. But Annie touched him and he did, he sent her to Perkins School for the Blind, which was out of state; he used his state's money to send her there. Unheard of, such an expense for such a person considered uneducable, unmanageable, but he did it because Annie touched him and gave him hope. And she went to the Perkins School for the Blind and there she touched the schoolmaster and the schoolmaster encouraged her and she excelled.

"And in that area, there was a wealthy captain and the wealthy captain had a deaf, dumb, and blind daughter that was bitter and angry and prone to rages. Alexander Graham Bell referred this wealthy captain to the Perkins School for the Blind. There the schoolmaster persuaded this wealthy captain to have blind Annie as the tutor for his daughter.

"The deaf, dumb, and blind girl was Helen Keller, little Annie was Annie Sullivan. The story of the interaction between Annie and Helen Keller was portrayed in *The Miracle Worker*. Annie touched her. The story before that, the story of Annie, is person touching person, causing change, giving hope.

Sergeant York, the story of Sergeant York was a story of change followed by hope.

"Jackie Thompson and Jerry Thompson met by chance over the phone. At that time Jackie was in a dark place, no self-esteem, abused, despaired, somehow Jerry touched her and in touching her changed her and gave her hope. Then Jackie touched him back, not physically—that will never be possible, but touched him and change began and hope began and you saw how that too went on, Jerry touching others.

"Now you heard a few days ago reference to the Crucifixion and there are references in the Bible in support of the death penalty. There are references in the Bible in support of life. In the Bible it's attributed to God that He said: 'Whomsoever shed a man's blood, by man his blood be shed. And an eye for an eye.'

"But the first case of life, punishment instead of death, came early. In Genesis 4:2-16: Cain had killed Abel and because he killed his brother, he was a marked man. Cain was afraid that the first person who saw his marking, killed him, and he got told that he shall not be killed, his punishment was exile.

"Sodom and Gomorrah; Abraham negotiated with God for mercy for those sinners.

"Jacob and Esau, Esau had the right, the Bible said, to kill Jacob, to free him of his birthright, instead Esau offered grace and mercy. You have to keep in mind other contextual things in the Bible; homosexuality was punished by death, polygamy was okay. A rebellious child was taken to the gates of the city and stoned to death; slavery was okay.

"Placed in isolation, the Bible doesn't prohibit the death penalty, the Bible doesn't—you can go either way by quoting isolated quotes in the message of it, that was early and then Jesus was born and what did He tell you? He started teaching a different way.

"In the Sermon on the Mount He gave you the Beatitudes. He, there talked about retaliation and He referred back to an eye for an eye and a tooth for a tooth and then He told them there was a different way. And He lived His life and then He was Crucified and after that came Resurrection. After that came the spreading of good news, person by person, touching people, changing people.

"If you look at the whole message, it's a message of change and it's a message that has to be applied in an ever-evolving changing society. The Bible is the history of mankind and his relationship with God. No longer is homosexuality punishable by death, it's a change in society.

"Bishop Gettelfinger recognized that and the competing messages are mercy and justice, justice in the concept of equal punishment; do to him what he did to others. But Bishop Gettelfinger wrote that mercy is not just biblically based, it's not just religion, that has meaning in our world today because of the way our society has advanced. And he points out there appears not only in the Bible, but in the dictionary, the first definition of mercy: compassion or leniency shown especially to an offender subject to one's power.

"Imprisonment rather than death imposed as a penalty for first-degree murder. And he says in today's world why mercy out-wins justice, the concept of an eye for an eye is because 'we can control people, we can punish them with incarceration, we can protect society by life imprisonment without the possibility of parole.' The prisons, the change, the technology, prosecutors often argue that the death penalty is like war, that we send people to kill to protect our society. They say that the death penalty is doing that. The death penalty is killing to protect society.

"Even in war when the enemy is reduced to our control, is incarcerated, is disarmed, is chained, we do not kill him. Self-defense, they argue, this is self-defense, society's defense. Self-defense the law requires, is an instant killing when you're in immediate danger, not when you're disarmed and chained and housed and barred. You don't have to kill, that is the concept of mercy in terms of competing it with their demand for justice, telling you that the justice is to do to him what was done to the victim.

"The message then we take and apply as we live it and the stories, all the stories, are person touching person, causing change, giving hope. You heard about Jackie and Jerry; change and hope.

"You did hear about Jerry talking to these kids, does God give him limitations in his human inflicted damage so he can somehow talk to troubled teenagers? How many people can do that? How important is that? Is that not some work, some value? If he touches one troubled child and turns him away from the path that he was on and that child touches another child who raises a child right and breaks the chain? Is that not some worth? Is that not some value?

"You have seen the crimes. Mr. Massa has talked to you about them. There is no excuse for them; no one is saying that there is. But if you execute Jerry Thompson for that, that is as bad, that is as equal. They're saying he did that and that is why he should be killed, show him no mercy, they were shown no mercy. If you kill that evil, if you kill that bad, you also kill the good, the possibility the change that has begun that could continue, the hope that he has given others and can still give them and then spread out in a ripple effect, as the person he touches and gives change and hope who can touch the next and the next. You kill that also.

"I am not asking you to turn away from the vicious and brutal nature of these crimes, I am asking you for mercy, I'm asking you to be different, I'm asking you to be better, I'm asking you to give the control, imprisonment you can control and protect, but you could let the good go on, you can punish and I am asking for mercy to be better, to be different. I am not asking you to ignore that these victims had people that loved them, people that needed them, people that are crying for them.

"You do know that there are people that love and need Jerry and are crying for him. They tell you, well he caused that, don't consider that, but you can stop it. You can punish and protect without causing more people to lose who they love and they need. Remember the Court's instructions, you had them at the beginning, you're going to have them again. Vengeance and retribution are not appropriate considerations.

"This is not an evaluation of who deserves more to win. Let's not forget about what was done, let's consider what can be done. It's not about what evil was done, what good can be done.

"I am asking you for life over death out of consideration of hope. I am asking you for life over death out of consideration of change. I am asking you for life over death because it is better. And that the death is not necessary for protection or punishment because the punishment of life in prison without the possibility of parole satisfies the protection and punishment aspect. The execution will satisfy the vengeance and retribution and you are told that it's not appropriate consideration.

"In the instructions you are told that there is—the death penalty is never mandatory, that you can consider anything, any reason. I'm asking for life over death because you can. You also have new information; you have new information about Mr. Percy, some of it. He can still say Jerry made me, Jerry told me, Jerry told me to lie to the police when Jerry was locked up in that cell in Illinois and I was out talking to the trooper.

"He made me, he made me not tell about the three people that were killed. He made me say it was my gun, he made me say I shot it in Texas. The garage, he said, had been overtaken, he could say Jerry was making me grow marijuana in there, he never said Jerry was making him shoot cocaine into his veins at the relevant time.

"And he cannot say Jerry told him to flunk two polygraphs, he cannot say Jerry made him do that. You also now know that contrary to what you were told, your decision last week would never ever have sent Jerry home. You can consider the new information and the instructions talk about how—residual or lingering doubt.

"The instructions also talk about the establishment of that [unintelligible] fact is beyond a reasonable doubt, that's the same standard, there's no standard to the way you process finding the mitigation, that's individual to each of you. There's not a standard for that, the standard beyond a reasonable doubt applies to them establishing their aggravating circumstances. The concept of residual or lingering doubt recognizes—United States Supreme Court and the Court's Instructions here recognize—that there is a space, there is a place, between beyond a reasonable doubt and absolute certainty.

"And when you consider the ultimate sanction of death, execution, the approach should take you to that place, to that space, it cannot. Lightning did not strike Mr. Percy before March 18th, 1992, Mr. Percy hired a lawyer, negotiated immunity, and saved his own skin. If and when lightning does strike him, Jerry should be alive not dead.

"The instructions also make it clear that this—this decision between death and life is individual, it's each of you, each of you must come to that decision individually. It is not a committee or a board that's forging a consensus on the allocation of resources or the setting of policy. It's an individual decision for each of you to make, each of you find a reason for life, that reason is sufficient.

"The law doesn't—because it recognizes that if your decision is for execution you will not be together as a group when that day comes, when you read about it, you'll be alone with your own thoughts. But each of you have to consider the mitigation, possibly the evidence of change, the evidence of hope, the possibility of more change than hope, the concept of mercy, of being better.

"Beginning in April, I went on vacation with my family and I was with my children as much as I could, preparing them for this trial when I would be away from them so much.

And I could not—what I didn't prepare them for—what I did not prepare them for was the stress of it, because I had never experienced it. I don't have the experience or abilities as these esteemed gentlemen have, and I could not prepare them for the enormity of that pressure, that stress, because I was not prepared for it. And I was thinking with all of my education and training I don't know how I have been able to keep standing up.

"And I sure don't know how Jerry, whose life is at stake, has been able to do it as well as he has. But I talked to my kids about what I do and my youngest, my nine-year -old, she calls my clients, 'my guys.' And one day I was telling her it's a death penalty case and I talked to her about how it is, what it is.

"And she said, 'Daddy, do they want to kill your guy?' I said, 'Well, honey, some people take it if something terrible and horrible was done to someone that the same thing should be done to that person.' She said, 'But does that make that right?' And I said, 'I don't think so, but some people do.'

"A child needs to know both sides, and I told her, 'And sometimes when people are murdered, killed, the people that they have been taken from think that it would help if we could enact the most extreme punishment of death for the person that did it. It will help them with their loss.'

"And she said, 'But won't they still be sad?' And I said, 'Yes, they will, and others will be sad too.' We also talked about the purpose, as considered by some, that if we kill people who kill it will stop other people from killing and she asked if that works and I said, 'No. From the beginning of time killing people who kill people has not stopped the killing.'

"There is human worth here and there is human value here, there is reason for mercy. Life imprisonment without parole satisfies the concerns for protection, it does punish and it punishes with recognition of change and hope and the possibility for more. I am asking you to spare his life. Thank you."

CHAPTER 31—END
THE BRUTALITY

Sells could not stomach the idea that Jerry Thompson could brutalize people his entire life and then gun down at least five innocent victims and live to brag about it. Hennessy's argument had been spellbinding, but if the jury wanted passion, Sells would bring them a mountain of it. He stood to face the jury.

"I am appalled at the suggestion that there is any comparison between the two young women Annie Sullivan and Helen Keller, who overcame seemingly insurmountable physical limitations to accomplish the miraculous, and Jerry Thompson, who was hell-bent on destroying the lives of all who stood in his way. Instead there is a stark contrast between the heights to which the human spirit can soar and the depths to which an evil mind can sink.

"Thompson had no regard for his fellow man. He had a scorched earth policy. Kill anyone who could inform on your murder and mayhem. His motto was 'No witnesses. No worries.' Thank God he had a lapse of judgment for he left alive one witness who sealed his fate. Doug Percy eventually summoned the courage and conscience to share his dark secret of Thompson's wanton destruction. Otherwise, who knows how long the trail of victims would have been?

"Mr. Hennessy has asked you to consider the impact on those whose lives he has touched before you impose the death penalty. And rightly you should. Mr. Hennessy argued that Thompson touched the lives of his mother, his brothers and sister, his daughters and those that he ministered to in prison. That Thompson touched the life of Jackie Thompson, his jailhouse bride. That she was spiritually in a dark place when Thompson connected with her. Must have been one hell of a dark place to require rescue by the Prince of Darkness.

"Mr. Hennessy said he is not asking you to ignore that the victims had people that loved them, people that needed them, people that are crying for them. Jerry Thompson 'reached out and touched' the lives of many when he brutally slaughtered Melvin Hillis, Robert Beeler, and Wesley Crandall. Their souls cry out for justice. Justice so Jerry Thompson cannot kill again. Justice so others do not feel the unbearable loss that so many have already felt.

"Mr. Massa and I stand before you with heavy heart and somber spirit. We realize what an awesome responsibility you must feel in making this soul-wrenching decision of whether to recommend that Jerry Thompson be put to death.

"I am not going to stand here and argue the Scriptures and quote chapter and verse as justification for what is being requested. There are at least two of you, probably more, that know the Bible better than I. I am not going to argue that Jerry Thompson should be sentenced to death because of passages in the Bible. But the Bible certainly does not forbid the death sentence in cases like this one.

"Your decision will help the prosecutors in this county and throughout this state decide under what circumstances the death penalty is appropriate. The death penalty is part of our laws. You heard the Court's instructions on the law. You will hear more instructions in that regard. You understand the difficult process that has to take place before you can even consider recommending that Thompson be put to death. You understand it painfully well because you all have sat through these excruciating proceedings.

"It is not easy to get to this point. It is not easy for me to stand up here and argue to you to take a fellow human being's life. But, Ladies and Gentlemen, if not this case when is the death penalty appropriate? If not him, who? You let us know whether or not you feel it is appropriate in this case and we will consider that when we determine in what cases it should be filed.

"In my opinion, your role in this death-penalty process is the most important role because you, the citizens of this community, tell us what you think is right, what just and merited punishment should be meted out to somebody who has committed the atrocious acts that this man has.

"But you are not alone in shouldering the responsibility for this decision. The Marion County Prosecutor's Office made the decision that the death penalty was appropriate in this case. Judge Walton-Pratt will duly consider the recommendation that you make, but she shares the responsibility, as well, in determining whether or not the death sentence should be imposed.

"You remember the Crime Lab forensic firearm's examiner Evan Thompson testifying about how he put the bullets and shell casings under a microscope when comparing them to determine if there is a match? Only when he is one hundred percent certain, will he come into court and testify that those bullets and shell castings came from a certain gun to the exclusion of all other guns in the world. Well, that microscopic examination pales in comparison to what will happen in this case should you recommend the death sentence and should the Judge order it."

Mr. Hennessy objected and the lawyers approached the bench. Defending attorneys Hennessy and Cleary complained that Sells was minimizing the role of the jury and that it violated a legal precedent. Sells argued that he was only telling the jury the truth and that what he was explaining was in their instructions anyway. The Court warned Sells not to cross the boundary line and overruled the objection.

Sells continued. "To assist you in your decision you have seen evidence of horrible crimes. You would probably think more of squashing a bug than Jerry Thompson did about killing his victims.

"You can consider the circumstances of the crimes. Weigh those against the mitigation evidence presented by the Defense of selected portions of Thompson's life.

"The testimony of Thompson's mother had to pull at your heart strings. It was shocking to hear the abuse that was suffered in that household at the hands of Jerry Thompson's father. That abuse touched everybody in that home. I asked her if anybody else turned into a killer. She said no.

"We were all petrified by what happened next. Thompson sprang out of his chair like an attacking grizzly bear and roared, 'Stop this! Stop this right now! I will not have my mother up there beggin' for my life for something I did not do.'

"Ladies and Gentlemen, you witnessed the true bestial nature of Jerry Thompson. And that was in this courtroom surrounded by several armed deputy sheriffs. If he could not control his baser instincts under those circumstances and knowing that his life was dependent on his best behavior, how could we expect he ever would?

"Defense witness Dr. Gelbort testified that Jerry Thompson had a defect of the frontal lobe of his brain that impaired his ability to be a leader or to mastermind criminal enterprises. That he felt Thompson could be controlled in a secure setting. He reluctantly acknowledged, however, that he could not assure us that Thompson would never kill again.

"No one is safe from the ravenous, predatory behavior of Jerry Thompson even in a prison setting. Should we expose prison guards to the violent threat Thompson poses? Or how about inmates in the general prison population, especially those who have a chance to reform and one day return to society? Should he be allowed to influence, corrupt, injure, or perhaps kill another inmate?

"What if, God forbid, he somehow escaped from prison? Should we have to assume that risk? Why should we have to worry about where he is or what he is doing? Society must be protected from this savage killer. We have an absolute right to feel safe from Jerry Thompson. And the only way we can be safe is if he is on Death Row awaiting execution.

"I know this cannot be an easy decision to reach, sentencing a fellow human being to death. But in your hearts and minds you know it must be done.

"That Tennessee fellow I talked about yesterday, Alvin York, grappled with the same monumental decision. After Alvin was struck by lightning, then found religion, he could not harm a fellow human being. Unfortunately for him, he was drafted into the Army during World War I. With his preacher's help, he attempted to obtain an exemption from military service as a conscientious objector because of his religious beliefs. The Army rejected his request. He was inducted into the Army and sent to basic training.

"His fellow soldiers were aware that he had tried to avoid the draft and rode him pretty hard, especially the sergeants. But Alvin eventually earned their respect because of his hard work and incomparable marksmanship. That Tennessee boy could really shoot.

"Alvin's commanding officer was also a man of strong spiritual beliefs. After a heart-to-heart talk with Alvin, he became convinced of the sincerity of Alvin's convictions. He gave Alvin a furlough to go back home for some soul-searching. If after that time, Alvin still felt he could not fight in the war, he would help Alvin secure an exemption from service.

"Alvin went back to his Tennessee hills and prayed to God for an answer. He took his Bible and his hound dog up the mountain to sort things out. He read that Bible for hours and finally fell asleep. Awakened by a gust of wind, he looked down at the open Bible on his lap. The wind blew the pages to the book of Matthew. A passage caught Alvin's attention. 'Render unto Caesar those things that are Caesar's and unto God those things that are God's.' Matthew 22: verse 21.

"Alvin pondered the significance of that verse. After much deliberation, he concluded that God was telling him that if man's law did not conflict with God's law, he should follow the law of man, the law of the United States of America. He also concluded that if he could shorten the war by using his shooting skill against the German army, he should do just that. By taking lives, he could thereby save lives.

"Alvin fought and shot many Germans because of his unerring marksmanship and exceptional courage. He was our nation's most decorated World War I hero and was awarded the Congressional Medal of Honor. Alvin saved lives by taking lives.

"Ladies and Gentlemen of the jury I am asking you to save lives by recommending that the life of Jerry Thompson be taken.

"I have a lovely wife and a beautiful ten-month-old daughter at home whom I have not seen much of the last few days, not nearly as much as I would like. I feel blessed to have them. One of these days I will have to explain to that little girl what I do for a living and why I came into a courtroom and asked you twelve people to sentence a man to die. I will tell her what I believe in my heart. I did it to protect her and her mother and others. And that is what I am asking you to do, to recommend that Jerry Thompson be sentenced to death to protect her, her mother and every other person he might 'reach out and touch.'

"May the Lord be with you."

CHAPTER 32—THE JURY DECIDES

Judge Tanya Walton-Pratt read to the jury the instructions on the law applicable to the case, including the tremendous legal burden on the State in making the necessary proofs in requesting the death sentence. They were told that even if the State had met that burden, the jurors were not required to recommend the death sentence, but if they did, their verdict must be unanimous. They then retired to the jury room to deliberate Jerry Thompson's fate. The process could take hours, days, even weeks.

Within two hours, the jury notified the Court that they had reached a verdict. That was a very quick verdict in a death penalty case. The jury did not even ask any questions during their deliberations. They always ask questions.

Larry Sells and Mark Massa were not sure what to make of the quick verdict. Two ministers had been left on the jury. From their answers during the jury selection process, it appeared they would be willing to fairly consider the death penalty. Several of Sells's peers had chastised him for leaving them on the jury, arguing that a minister was not likely to impose a death sentence. Sells went with his gut instinct. He believed they would "pull the trigger" on Thompson. Now he began to question those instincts.

Jerry Thompson, David Hennessy, and Joseph Cleary were standing at the Defense table when the court bailiff led the jury to their seats in the jury box. The defendant and his attorneys appeared optimistic. After all, Hennessy had performed masterfully. No jury could unanimously agree to recommend death after his persuasive final argument just a short time before. Their relaxed demeanor indicated they believed Thompson's life had been spared.

Larry Sells, Mark Massa, and Kathy Cronley stood anxiously at the Prosecutor's table awaiting the final outcome of what had been a very contentious and nerve-wracking trial. They felt they had worked very hard and had done their best in presenting the State's case against Jerry Thompson. But was their best good enough? They would soon find out.

The bailiff collected the verdict form from the jury foreman and delivered it to Judge Tanya Walton-Pratt. This was her first death penalty case. She had acquitted herself admirably dealing with complex issues and, at times, a tumultuous atmosphere, especially after Thompson's explosive outburst. She had been impartial throughout the proceedings providing the Defense and the State a fair trial even though David Hennessy was a close friend and even though she did not favor the death penalty.

She carefully examined the verdict form. Then, before a hushed courtroom packed with prosecutors, defense attorneys, and loved ones of the victims and loved ones of Thompson, Judge Walton-Pratt announced, "We, the jury, recommend that Jerry Thompson be sentenced to death."

The Judge polled the jurors to make certain that each individual juror had reached that verdict, and each juror responded that he or she had. She thanked the jurors then excused them and set a future date for the actual imposition of sentence.

Larry Sells was in a fog of euphoria and did not observe most of those courtroom activities. He had experienced such a rush of adrenaline that he could have rolled Sisyphus's boulder up the hill. Actually, he had already accomplished that feat, considering all of the legal obstacles that had to be overcome to get this far. Outwardly, he attempted to maintain some sense of dignity and decorum. He accepted congratulations from his colleagues and heartfelt thanks from the Hillis and Beeler family members. They did not have their loved ones back but they had received justice in the courtroom. They did not feel good. They never would. But they felt better.

Sells glanced at the defendant and his lawyers. Initially, Thompson displayed no emotion. Hennessy and Cleary appeared devastated, but quickly recovered their equilibrium and were consoling their client. Probably telling him they were going to win his case on appeal. They had done it three years before.

But Thompson was not responding to their overtures. His mood soon changed dramatically. His coal black eyes radiated visceral hatred. The murderous psychopath directed his rage toward Sells, the man he blamed for his conviction.

Thompson, the same man who had refused to appear for the penalty phase of his first trial in 1996 because Sells called him names, was ready to take Sells apart limb from limb. One thing stood in his way. Not the sheriff deputies. They were too distant to stop him. No, it was the handcuffs, belly chains, and leg irons that he still wore.

Sells smiled at him, winked and mouthed the words, "Got you again, big boy!"

In a way, Sells experienced a slight pang of guilt over feeling so good about playing a part in someone's future execution. But that temporary guilt passed rather quickly. He had done the right thing.

Judge Walton-Pratt had followed the jurors back to the jury room, where they went to collect their personal effects before heading to their homes. She again expressed her sincere appreciation for their services. Mark Massa, Kathy Cronley, and Larry Sells went back to the room shortly thereafter to thank them as well. As they entered, they were greeted with a hearty applause. Besides feeling somewhat embarrassed, Sells was actually speechless for the first time since the trial had begun.

The jurors were friendly with each other and with the Prosecution team. They expressed no regrets especially after Sells informed them of all the other crimes and murders that Thompson had committed.

They felt that he had done more than what they heard about, but what they had heard was more than sufficient cause for their decision. The ordeal of the trial they had just completed had brought them closer together. It could have easily made them mortal enemies.

One of the preachers told Sells in the presence of his fellow jurors that before they had voted on whether to recommend the death sentence, they joined hands and prayed for guidance. Following the prayer, they agreed that the death penalty was the only appropriate sentence.

At the end of his final argument, the last thing Sells had told the jurors was, "May the Lord be with you." And he was.

CHAPTER 33—DEATH ROW

On September 29, 2000, over nine-and-one-half years after Jerry Thompson had taken the lives of Melvin Hillis and Robert Beeler, Thompson was sentenced to death by lethal injection by Judge Tanya Walton-Pratt in accordance with the jury verdict and pursuant to statute. The execution was scheduled to take place in a year, again as prescribed by statute.

But everybody knew that would not happen. It would be another ten to fifteen years before all the legal proceedings and appeals were exhausted and Thompson could meet the Grim Reaper, if he ever did.

The courts would probably once again find some way to set aside the conviction. With each passing year, murdering psychopaths became increasingly more heinous, and homicides increased significantly, while the courts became less inclined to impose the ultimate sanction, as did jurors.

During jury selection in Thompson's first trial in 1996, Larry Sells encountered a prospective juror who was against the death penalty. This, in and of itself, was not unusual but the circumstances were perplexing. This potential juror had completed a very detailed questionnaire as to his background and beliefs, as had all the other people summoned for jury service in the case. Sells thought the Defense-prepared questionnaire very intrusive, but the Court permitted it.

This particular man had revealed that he had fought for his country in the Korean War. Sells could not understand why this man, one who had fought in a war against an evil regime, would not impose the death sentence if the murders were proved. The man in his late sixties still had a military bearing and commanding presence.

He looked Sells right in the eye and in a strong voice said, "If you prove this man did what you charged him with, and we find him guilty, he should straightway be taken out of this courthouse and hung in the nearest tree. But you won't do that so I am against the death penalty."

Sells asked, "Shouldn't he be entitled to an appeal of his conviction?"

"No. No appeal. If we find him guilty, just take him out and hang him."

Sells responded, "Can't say I disagree with you, sir. Thank you for your military service and your candor here today." The Defense could not wait to send this military veteran packing.

Thompson was shipped off to Death Row, but Sells was not confident that Thompson would ever really pay for his crimes. He was also concerned that he might hurt or kill someone in prison, or find some way to escape. Then come after Sells and his family.

But two years later something unbelievable happened and neither Larry Sells nor anybody else had to worry anymore. On October 27, 2002, Jerry Thompson, the killer, was slain by other killers!

On that date, Jerry Thompson was found dead in the recreation area of a cellblock on "X Row" (Death Row) at the Indiana State Prison in Michigan City, Indiana. Thompson suffered several fatal stab wounds. At the time, Thompson's conviction was on direct appeal to the Indiana Supreme Court.

Thompson had been executed, not by the State, but by other Death Row inmates. He was surrounded by other killers and stabbed thirty times.

Larry Sells was not displeased with the news. On October 29, 2002, Sells sent a message to Homicide Detective David Phillips and others in the law enforcement community with the subject line: Execution of Jerry Thompson. His message:

Last Saturday Jerry Thompson was executed somewhat ahead of schedule by fellow Death Row inmates at the Indiana State Prison. Thompson was convicted in 1996 (John Commons and I prosecuted the case) for the 1991 Robbery and Murders of Melvin Hillis and Robert Beeler. Criminal Court 3 Judge John R. Barney "reluctantly" (Ha! Ha!) followed the jury's recommendation and imposed the death sentence. The Indiana Supreme Court "enthusiastically" (no Ha! Ha!) reversed the conviction. In 2000 Mark Massa and I retried the case in Criminal Court 1 with the same result. Thompson's executioners, having little confidence in the criminal justice system and the Indiana Supreme Court doing the right thing, "flushed" Thompson from this world.

Thompson's death was the first fatal attack among Death Row inmates in at least fifteen years.

Before his untimely death (it should have come much, much sooner), forty-one-year-old Jerry Thompson had been confined a total of approximately twenty-three years for a variety of offenses, including Theft, Robbery, Child Molestation, and, of course, Murder. During a six-month period in 1991, Thompson killed at least five people. In this morning's *Indianapolis Star*, David Hennessy, who represented Thompson in the 2000 trial, was quoted as saying he found some "goodness" in Thompson and was soliciting donations to bury Thompson in the family plot. Please! *Star* did not print my quotes.

"This STONE COLD, HEARTLESS, SOULLESS KILLER wreaked havoc, death, destruction, excruciating and permanent pain and suffering to all those unfortunate souls that he 'reached out and touched.' Saturday, HE was 'TOUCHED,' thirty times by three shivs!

"…they that take the sword shall perish with the sword." Matthew 26:52

"Jerry Thompson won his first appeal and very well may have prevailed again but for Saturday's events. But I bet he does not fare so well with his next appeal before the ALMIGHTY!

"'Dust to dust, ashes to ashes. The Lord giveth; the Lord taketh away. Blessed be the name of the Lord.' Clint Eastwood in *The Outlaw Josey Wales* (quoting from the book of Job in the Bible)."

Douglas Percy died of natural causes on July 20, 2009.

CHAPTER 34—WHO KILLED THOMPSON?

May 4, 2000

Mr. Scott C. Newman Esquire

Marion County Prosecutor

200 East Market Street, Suite 560

Indianapolis, Indiana 46204

Sir,

I am writing to commend the outstanding performance of Mark Massa and Larry Sells during the just complete trial of Jerry Thompson. Their combined efforts secured the conviction of one of the most brutal killers I have ever encountered. It is a testament to their knowledge and skill that they were able to do this after the Indiana Supreme Court reversed Thompson's earlier conviction and placed restrictions on the evidence available to the State. Mr. Sells and Mr. Massa are exemplary advocates for the citizens of this county. You should have pride in having such men on your staff.

One of the best measures of success is the skill of one's adversaries. In this case Mr. Massa and Mr. Sells faced David Hennessy and Joseph Cleary, both well-respected lawyers and renowned opponents of the death penalty. Mr.

Cleary apparently handled the research and writing involved in the defense with Mr. Hennessy handling the bulk of the in-court proceedings. Mr. Hennessy is a well-prepared, skilled and quick-thinking defense attorney. His reputation for mounting a pugnacious and effective defense of his clients is both wide-spread and well deserved.

After three days of contentious jury selection the trial began. By midday Thursday Mr. Sells and Mr. Massa had correctly anticipated the defense strategy of Mr. Hennessy and Mr. Cleary. They adapted the State's presentation of witnesses and evidence accordingly, throwing the defense team into such confusion that Mr. Hennessy bitterly complained to Judge Walton-Pratt that he had been hamstrung and needed a continuance to regroup. This occurred despite the veritable who's who of defense attorneys and death penalty mitigation experts who regularly attended the trial and who were providing assistance and information to Thompson's defense team.

Mr. Hennessy littered his defense with potential pitfalls that, if not recognized and properly countered, would form the basis for later appeals or that would allow he and Mr. Cleary to request a mistrial. At each juncture Mr. Massa and Mr. Sells correctly saw the traps and effectively evaded them. Their performance was masterful.

Following Thompson's conviction on all charged counts Mr. Sells and Mr. Massa presented the jury with the information required in the penalty phase. Their delivery was succinct, again preventing Mr. Cleary and Mr. Hennessy from using the State's case to further their own.

The defense then began calling mitigation witnesses. The skill and quick-witted cross-examination of these witnesses by Mr. Massa and Mr. Sells blunted their effect upon the jury. In some instances, information beneficial to the State's case was elicited from the defendant's own witnesses. A neuropsychologist called by the defense admitted under cross-examination that nothing in his testing and evaluation would allow him to assure anyone, even after identifying a frontal lobe deficiency in the defendant and prescribing treatment for that condition, that Jerry Thompson would never kill again. That was a powerful moment that was not lost on the jurors.

Mr. Massa and Mr. Sells presentation of this case led the jurors to recommend the court sentence for Jerry Thompson to die for his heinous and cold-blooded crimes. This is a just verdict that would not have been rendered absent the dedicated advocacy of Mr. Sells and Mr. Massa on behalf of the citizens of our community. They deserve any accolades you may have at your disposal.

Sincerely,

Sergeant David E. Phillips

Indianapolis Police Department

Homicide Branch, Homicide Unit Supervisor

***

Alpha Funeral Services at 3925 East New York Street was hired to provide a simple service for Jerry Thompson. Funeral director Tony Edwards advised Jackie Thompson against seeing the body. "I'd explain he simply isn't viewable at this point," Edwards told the widow. She opted for a closed casket.

Although Jerry was on Death Row, Jackie had not been prepared to plan a funeral. "I'd always felt he would be exonerated," she said. But the service was necessary. Jerry had confided to Jackie that his great fear was fire. In Indiana, inmates can be buried on the prison grounds at no cost to the family but are cremated first.

Inmates' families are allowed to attend graveside services following the cremation, but afterward, the cemetery is off limits to them. This was not acceptable to Jackie. *Indianapolis Star* reporter Will Higgins quoted the widow as saying that there was no way she'd allow her husband to be consumed by flames and spend eternity behind the fence.

Although Jackie had no wealth and lived on Social Security disability benefits, she insisted that her husband would be buried.

The funeral was an economical one. There was a graveside service with no calling hours. On November 1 at 2:00 p.m., Jerry Thompson was buried in Anderson Cemetery near the home of his wife, Jacqueline L. Guy Thompson. Appeals were made to the public to help fund the $2,700 in funeral costs.

Jerry's attorneys, David Hennessy and Joe Cleary paid for the funeral. Higgins wrote that Jackie Thompson "contemplates suing the Department of Correction for failing to protect her husband."

***

Death Row at the Indiana State Prison in Michigan City is a stark, steel and concrete structure built to contain those convicts society most fears. Each cell is a stage play where three walls are the room and the fourth wall is open to the audience. Privacy, even on the toilet, is a luxury lost for life and the bunks could pass for a mortician's slab. When the priest visits to offer prayer or Communion, he must pass the Host between thick, powerful bars.

Twenty-two-year-old "Iceman" Kevin A. Conner made his home on Death Row on November 3, 1988. Over his stay he acquired a television and a small library of books, mostly philosophy and science fiction. He spent eighteen years locked down before his execution by lethal injection on July 27, 2005. His death was payment for a wild night with the boys.

On January 26, 1988, Conner was at the home of Tony Moore, age twenty-four, and two other nineteen-year-old acquaintances, Steve Wentland and Bruce Voge. Wentland and Moore went for a drive and Conner rode in the backseat. Wentland and Moore argued and Moore struck Wentland with Conner's knife. Wentland fled from the car but Moore ran him down with the automobile. Then Conner got out, beat Wentland with his fists and stabbed him more than a dozen times.

Conner and Moore then went to a business in the 1600 block of Deloss Street. There, they awakened Conner's boss to get keys to a warehouse. Inside the warehouse, Conner and Moore argued about what to do. Conner's boss was reawakened by the blast of a sawed-off shotgun. Conner told his boss he had to off Tony. He got help from friends to remove the body and returned to Moore's home where he again used the shotgun to end Voge's life as he slept on the couch.

Kevin Conner fled to Texas. He was captured in Amarillo on a bus headed for California and returned to Indiana to stand trial. His Defense attorneys pled for leniency. Conner was intoxicated and just twenty-two years old at the time. He had suffered the loss of his father. He was genuinely remorseful and had no significant history of criminal conduct. He loved to write and to draw. He had been generous in helping pay rent for his girlfriend.

But Conner's victims were also young and had lives before them. Conner was convicted of all three deaths and sentenced to sixty years for Wentland's death and received the death penalty for each of the two shotgun murders.

As the clock ticked toward his moment of execution, Conner sent a statement to Indiana Governor Mitch Daniels, asking not to be pardoned. He said, "…killing a person is far more honest and humane than imposed repression under the guise of justice in the penal system." He told reporters, "I've got no desire to grow old in prison."

A week before his execution, Conner confessed to stabbing Jerry Thompson to death during a recreation period. Six other prisoners were present when Thompson died and it has been speculated that all seven of the group ganged up to take the giant down. His body, bearing several fatal stab wounds, was found on October 27, 2002, in the recreation area of a cellblock on "X Row." When he died, he was on direct appeal from his death sentence following a retrial in Marion County, Indiana. The death penalty found him at the hands of others like himself. Killers.

Conner was known for his interests in writing and drawing. He sent an ink drawing of Bugs Bunny and Yosemite Sam to his sister, a final gift to his niece.

He watched a dark comedy on Showtime, *Dead Like Me*, a parody of a team of grim reapers. His final feast came from Dairy Queen: four chili dogs, onion rings, a banana split, and an Oreo blizzard. He spent his final hours calling friends and relatives while smoking two cigars. He did not ask for a spiritual advisor and he said he was proud of killing Thompson.

The group of death penalty protesters outside the gate were diminished by steady rain.

"I'm not bugging about it," Conner had said. "What is there to be afraid of? It's an inevitable fact that at some point you have to die." Conner's final words, peppered with profanity, were, "Everybody has to die sometime, so...let's get on with the killing."

ADDITIONAL NOTES

Between 1959 and 1974, the Thompson family reportedly moved over twenty-two times. Most of their homes were rat infested, many had an outhouse but no plumbing, and several were one- or two-room dwellings.

In the early 1970s Sara Thompson went on disability due to rheumatoid arthritis and her extreme weight, which topped 400 pounds. She managed to lose the weight but never returned to work. She and Marvin divorced on May 25, 1973, but continued to live together until Marvin's death in 1992.

Dann Brothers Junkyard was Marvin's only listed place of employment. Jerry was arrested twice for robbing Dann's. On October 23, 1979, he was caught stealing a mini bike and car parts. On September 11, 1981, he stole cast iron.

Most of Jerry Thompson's referrals to Juvenile Courts regarded events that happened while Jerry Thompson was in the company of older youths, especially his older brother, David. An investigator who perused Thompson's juvenile records noted that, "There is no indication from review of the Henry County Juvenile Court Records of concerns regarding the condition of the home or of the parents other than a statement that, 'children lacked parental supervision because the mother works.'"

A few weeks after his twelfth birthday, Jerry Kevin Thompson damaged a residence, a church, and a trailer. He was charged with vandalism and truancy. He was counseled on an informal basis and he paid restitution. Problem solved. Almost.

Within a year he was apprehended three more times and charged with truancy, being a runaway, and being incorrigible. Each time he was referred to Juvenile Probation and placed in Informal Adjustment. Basically, he was told to go back to the violent hellhole that was his home and behave himself.

Thompson related that his parents divorced when he was thirteen years old and described his mother as the primary disciplinarian in the home. He said that at the hands of his father and uncles he was abused on all levels: mentally, physically, and sexually "as far back as I can remember." He denied ever receiving medical treatment or counseling as a result of the abuse.

Sara Thompson described herself as the primary parent. She said that her husband drank and gambled and was chronically in and out of prison.

April 10, 1973. Charged with Vandalism and Truancy, "Jerry's case was handled informally and referred to counseling." Counseling sessions, expected to address Jerry's anger problems, were discontinued by his mother after three sessions.

July 17, 1974. Jerry and some other youths were caught shooting out the windows of a local business. He and the other children were ordered to make restitution.

Thompson attended New Castle High School-North Campus but did not graduate. He also attended Warren Central High School and later earned his GED. He had taken Ivy Tech classes at the Indiana State Prison in Michigan City, Indiana. He had referrals for mental problems, physical problems, and alcohol and drug abuse.

When asked if he was abused by his father, Jerry said no. He did state, however, "that his father would backhand him for no reason."

The Thompson family was not involved in the community or any church. Jerry wanted to be involved in sports, but was unable to.

February 16, 1977. According to a background presentencing report: "Jerry was charged with battery and failure to leave school grounds." He received a "suspended commitment to the Indiana Boy's School and ordered to reside with his brother Stephen in Indianapolis." He was required to attend school while staying with Stephen. He completed one semester at Warren Central High School and then enlisted in the National Guard. "There is no indication that Jerry was courtesy supervised by the Marion County Probation Department while living in Indianapolis."

Jerry stayed in Indianapolis with Steve for nine months. He went to Fort Knox with the National Guard and was discharged three months later. Then he went to live with David in Muncie.

Pamela Binge, Jerry's Indiana Boys' School orientation counselor, described the teenaged Jerry as evasive, depressed, and hostile. He "blames others for his misfortunes, and tends to negate the seriousness of his past behaviors," Binge reported.

She found him angry and reluctant to maintain eye contact with those in authority. "He claims he has no family problems," the counselor said. "He is manipulative, tries to convince you that he was really a victim of circumstances." She said he needed to grow up and accept responsibility for his actions. She found his intelligence to be average to above average.

All three of Jerry's brothers had been committed to Indiana Boys' School. All the Thompson children ran away from home and were chronically truant from school. When Jerry was released from Boys' School, he found himself without an anchor. He had no vocational skills and no support from his family or the community.

Jerry's sister, Susan Diane Thompson Ballenger, pregnant with her son, left home at age sixteen after Marvin sexually assaulted her. She moved to Richmond, Indiana, and completed high school. Working full time, she completed a four-year nursing degree at Indiana University East and then went to work at Reid Memorial Hospital in New Castle.

During the three months he served in the National Guard in 1978, Jerry Thompson received awards for grenade, rifle, and handgun marksmanship. At Fort Knox, Kentucky, Thompson worked as a field track mechanic. Numerous bones were broken in Jerry Thompson's hand when a master link for a tank track fell on his hand. He was discharged because the injury rendered him incapable of shooting guns.

Upon returning to New Castle, Thompson became involved in criminal activity and was incarcerated for a period of two years in the Pendleton Reformatory.

Jerry Thompson served time in the Indiana State Reformatory in 1980, and also 1982–1984. He described himself at that time as "naive and fearful and was easily swayed by peer pressure to join a gang." He said he "shunned gang involvement during subsequent incarcerations."

Thompson said his interests and leisure activities included football, boxing, writing, and building cars and motorcycles. He was a third-degree black belt in karate. His occupational skills include welding, auto mechanics, plumbing, and electrical work. He stated no religious affiliation but said he did believe in God and that he read the Bible. His religious experience included Agnosticism, Norse Theology, and Pentecostal Christianity.

His life had changed since he met his wife, Jackie, Thompson said. She helped him with religion and he had been involved with the Reverend Dave Clemens of the Chaplain's Office at the Marion County Jail, with Project Hope and Scared Straight programs. In Johnson County he was involved in Choose to Change. In the Marion County Jail, he reportedly spoke with children about his experience and said he wanted to teach others about his life. He said he wanted to keep children from becoming like him.

November 13, 1984. Thompson was sentenced to seven years for Child Molest. The victim was the twelve-year-old daughter of a former girlfriend. The charges stated that, "Jerry allegedly had the child fondle him while in a shower." He was sent to the Indiana State Prison in Michigan City from February 4, 1986, to August 16, 1988.

Before his sentencing, Thompson was found to be in good health and coherent in his thought processes. He had scars, though, from his life on the streets.

About age twenty-eight, he interjected himself in a squabble where a man in a car was shaking a teenage girl. The man caught the end of Thompson's nose on a shotgun sight, tearing the end of it. He repaired the wound with a butterfly clip.

He has also had broken bones in his nose, ankle, and collarbone.

Bullet wounds also left scars, although Thompson sought no medical attention for the wounds and never reported who his assailants were. In 1984 he was shot in the right leg with a .22 caliber handgun. The bullet fell out of his leg and he treated the wound himself. In 1990 he was shot in the left hip. He said he removed the bullet himself with a hemostat. Four days later his lower back was grazed by another bullet. In 1991, after stealing a bicycle from a garage, Thompson was shot in the shoulder.

During incarceration Thompson was stabbed with an ice pick and hit with a pipe and a brick. He received medical treatment from the Indiana Department of Corrections for those wounds.

Thompson admitted that he had used drugs, including alcohol, marijuana, and cocaine, but claimed he was not an addict. Despite earlier reports of his father's drunken behavior, Thompson now stated that his father *used alcohol, but that his father was not abusive and was able to maintain his alcohol consumption.* Thompson stated that he himself began drinking at age fifteen.

In a later interview, Thompson recanted these statements and said that his father was abusive and could not control himself under the influence of alcohol. He said he himself had used numerous drugs including marijuana, cocaine, heroin, PCP, acid, and crack. As a young teen, fishing with his father and brother David, Thompson said he would black out from the combination of beer and Dark Eyes vodka.

***

Condemned killer Kevin A. Conner, age forty, said that he killed Thompson and was proud of what he did. "Police had dubbed Conner 'Iceman' for his cold demeanor." (*Indianapolis Star* article by Vic Ryckaert)

Thompson's eldest daughter was Crystal Holly Thompson, born November 11, 1980, to Dana Williams. She resided in New Castle, held two jobs, and had never used alcohol or drugs. Thompson had not seen his daughter during his incarceration but they maintained contact by mail. Thompson spoke proudly of his daughter and seemed to be well informed about the events in her life.

Shawn McCormick gave birth to Jerri Nicole Thompson on February 15, 1992. Shawn had custody of the child. Thompson had never seen her because he was incarcerated when she was born.

PHOTOS

Jerry Thompson Age 1 (Circa 1961)

STATE OF INDIANA   )   IN THE MARION COUNTY SUPERIOR COURT
) SS: CRIMINAL DIVISION, ROOM ONE
COUNTY OF MARION   )   THE HONORABLE TANYA WALTON PRATT, JUDGE

STATE OF INDIANA   )

  v.   **FILED** CAUSE NO. 49G01-9204-CF-060651

               MAY 03 2000

JERRY THOMPSON   ) *Sarah M. Taylor*
                    CLERK

RECOMMENDATION

"We the Jury, recommend the death penalty be imposed upon the Defendant, Jerry K. Thompson."

_____
FOREPERSON

"We the Jury, recommend life imprisonment without possibility of parole be imposed upon the Defendant, Jerry K. Thompson."

N/A
_____
FOREPERSON

"We, the Jury, recommend that neither the death penalty nor life imprisonment without the possibility of parole be imposed on the Defendant, Jerry K. Thompson."

N/A
_____
FOREPERSON

DATED: 5/3/2000

I certify that the alternate jurors have not taken part in Jury deliberations.

_____
FOREPERSON

Jury Verdict

Thompson Family (Circa 1978) Jerry and Father
"Hoggy" (on right), brothers and mother

Houses Jerry lived in as a child. None had
indoor plumbing. New Castle, IN

Doug Percy Mugshot (Circa 1992)

Jerry Thompson Mugshot (Circa 1992)

Deputy Prosecutor Larry Sells (Circa
2000). Final argument tie.

BACK TO HIS CELL: Convicted killer Jerry Thompson is escorted back to jail after court.

Jury recommends death

Jerry Thompson Led from Courtroom After Verdict

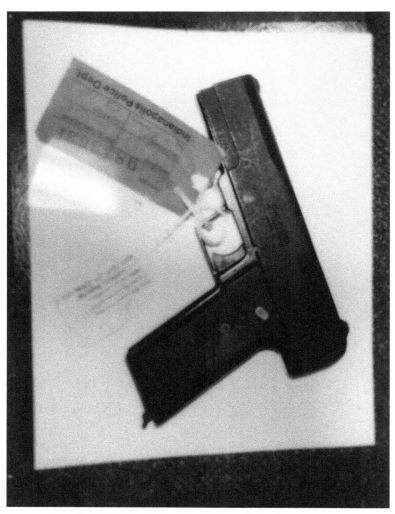

State's Exhibit 1 Stallard 9mm Murder Weapon

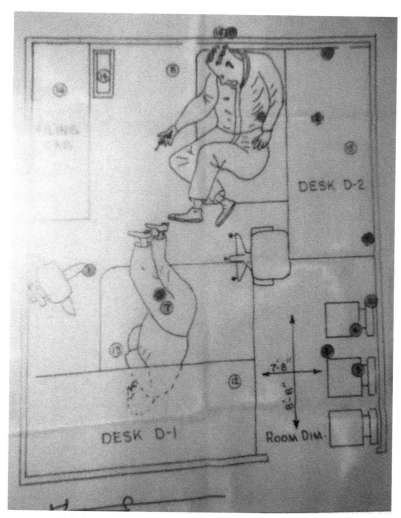

Trial Diagram of the Hillis Auto Sales Office

Hillis Auto Sales Sign

Hillis Auto Sales Building March 14, 1991

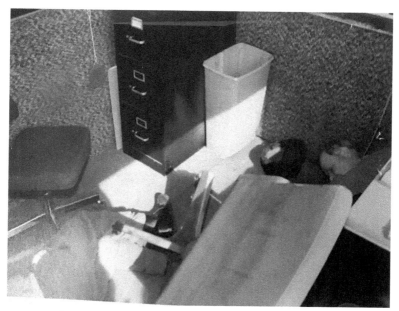

Hillis Auto Sales Office. Robert Beeler on left,
Melvin Hillis on right. March 14, 1991

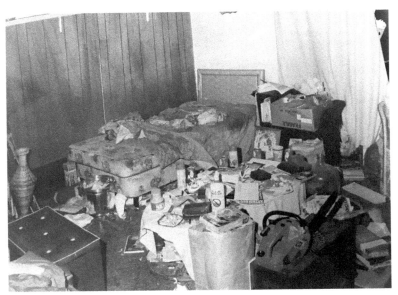

Wesley Chandler's Bedroom. February 14, 1991

Wesley Chandler House. February
14, 1991. New Castle, IN

Wesley Chandler Murder Scene in
Kitchen. February 14, 1991

For More News About Larry Sells and Margie Porter, Signup For Our Newsletter:

http://wbp.bz/newsletter

Word-of-mouth is critical to an author's long-term success. If you appreciated this book please leave a review on the Amazon sales page:

http://wbp.bz/beastofnewcastlea

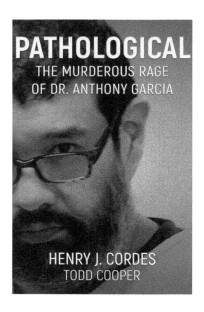